MW01001437

Through the stories of seventeen individuals we are given the gift of experience and wisdom demonstrating the power of mindful engagement and altruism to change not only our own lives but the lives of those around us. This book is an explosion of grace and enlightenment.

—*James R. Doty, MD, Director of CCARE, Stanford University*

With both sensitivity and boldness, Dr. Wendy Wood and Dr. Thaïs Mazur examine the nature and quality of collective social and environmental responsibility. The reader is called upon to search deeply within about how his or her own experiences might be shaped by these qualities of meaningful engagement and altruism, thus asking the profound question: What is required to truly *Do No Harm*?

—*Integral Publishers*

If you care about the world, then this is a must read!

—*Joan Jiko Halifax, Abbot, Upaya Zen Center*

Do No Harm is the perfect medicine for what ails the world today. In this book, Wendy and Thaïs elegantly articulate the elusive balance between the responsibility of sovereign individuals and the cooperative potential of collective awareness. And it's a great read, including beautiful stories and practical advice.

—*Duncan Autrey, Host of Fractal Friends Podcast, Democracy Politics and Conflict Engagement Initiative*

Into our troubled world, where differences more readily give rise to conflict than to mutual reverence, comes this gem of a book. Read it only if you are open to becoming a more enlightened human being.

—*Marilyn Lacey, Founder and
Executive Director of Mercy Beyond Borders*

The stories offer many insights and questions we all need to consider as we try to live our lives to help work for justice and peace and environmental sanity.

—*David Hartsough, Peaceworkers*

Wood and Mazur showcase repeatedly in this book, sometimes people's best efforts and most humane causes can actually produce new struggles and cause harm. Hardly anyone who causes conflict in the world does so knowingly and often does so with the best of intentions. This book attempts, and largely succeeds, in not only examining the global need for collective and progressive improvement but in also managing to provide the reader with the tools needed to improve the circle of humanity that revolves around them. Told in a series of detailed and in-depth interviews, this book not only encourages participation, it also provides so many powerful insights to move the reader towards a more mindful approach to life. Brilliant, richly told, and openly hopeful, this is a book that any world weary person can take comfort in.

—*Manhattan Book Review*

The range of contributors in this book is gratifying: a neuroscientist who works with and for traumatized children, a 'guerilla midwife' whose work it is to assist in delivering babies in environmental disaster zones and warzones, mediators and wisdom teachers. The importance of language, and particularly stories, is a common theme. Terms like compassion, mindfulness, and humility occur throughout, and *Do No Harm* offers inspiration for all those who respond to those key values. In that sense it can complement nonviolence and nonviolent action, and is a welcome addition.

—*Michael Nagler The Metta Center for Nonviolence, Founder and President*

Consolidating thousands of years of human techniques for supporting others and fostering change, while doing no harm, is no easy task. Wood and Mazur have done it with great skill in the book *Do No Harm*. If you work with and support people in conflict, drop everything, get this book and read it cover to cover. This "how to" book has nothing to do with lists or charts or secret methodologies. It goes much deeper as it lands you right smack dab in the middle of understanding your own deepest ways of interacting so you don't unintentionally make things worse. Front and center on my shelf of books for making change, and resolving organizational conflicts is Wood and Mazur's *Do No Harm*. This work is a solid touchstone for those of us who work to support positive culture, engagement, and good interpersonal relationships, and don't want to make things worse through our involvement.

—*Mark Batson Baril, Founder of San Francisco USA based Resologics*

In the midst of all that is going on in the world and as we struggle make our way through difficult situations, this book gives us some good insights into how to respond when faced with challenges and with the desire to show up the best way we can.

—*Richard Grayson, Veterans for Peace*

DO NO HARM

MINDFUL ENGAGEMENT
FOR A WORLD IN CRISIS

WENDY WOOD & THAÏS MAZUR

RioKai
PRESS

P. O. Box 443, Mendocino, CA 95460

RioKai Press
P. O. Box 443
Mendocino, CA 95640

Do No Harm: Mindful Engagement for a World in Crisis
2nd Edition

ISBN: 978-0-9980081-6-5

Library of Congress Control Number: 2016941445

Cover and Interior Design by Angela Tannehill-Caldwell

Editing by Rose-Anne Moore

CONTENTS

THE QUALITIES, STORIES AND PRACTICES OF MINDFUL ENGAGEMENT

PREFACE

It was a blistering hot midsummer morning, already over 100 degrees. The small desert town was quiet, as usual, when an old car pulled over to the side of the road and the driver's door flew open. A young woman fell to the ground, semi-conscious, and three little girls, ages 5, 8, and 11, jumped out of the car. They surrounded their mother who was lying unresponsive on the hot pavement. Calling out to her, they stood there, helpless and in tears. Moments later, another young girl, age 9, was leaving the only general store in town and, glancing over, saw the little girls and their mom. She came running over, stood there for a second, and said, "I know what to do. Wait here." She ran back into the store and returned with a big bag of ice. Standing over the woman on the ground, she opened the bag and poured the crushed ice on top of her. She then ran back and forth into the store for several more bags of ice until the woman regained consciousness. The girls and their mom had traveled from the Santa Clara Valley in California on their way to New Mexico. The heat of that desert morning had taken a toll. Heat prostration, a life threatening condition, was not uncommon for locals and travelers, and ice was the answer.

This is our shared story. Thaïs was the 5 year old whose mother collapsed, and Wendy was the 9 year old who saved her life. And yet, it wasn't until a casual conversation one afternoon, many many years later, that we realized we were bound together by this story.

Why have we shared this? Stories are in many ways what connects us to the soul of who we are. They are a uniquely human experience, and no two stories are alike—not even our own.

Our stories change as we change. They change as we contemplate them or as we enter into dialogue with others where our stories, as well as theirs, are being played out in conversations and interactions. Stories help us make sense of the world, allowing us to pay attention to what is important, what works, where we have struggled, and what actions we need to take. Our story is the perfect example of what we know to be true— what happens to you, happens to me, and what happens to me, happens to you. We are in this together.

In our professional lives we have worked with perpetrators and victims of the 1994 Rwandan genocide sitting in the same room, striving to renew and rebuild their trust in each other and restoring their hope for the future. We have watched female refugees in Bosnia finding their own ways to heal through dancing and singing, reclaiming their culture and their dignity lost to the tragedies of war. We have also seen deeds gone awry as well-intentioned groups and individuals attempt to intervene in social and environmental catastrophes. Certainly, no one enters their work with the intention to cause problems or create a bigger mess than when they started; however, we all know this occurs.

Yet, through decades of our professional work, we have repeatedly observed individuals, community groups, and organizations unknowingly cause harm, sometimes with lasting effects: an entire team of health care providers unwilling to address the deep emotional and spiritual suffering of an inmate while he lies dying in a hospital; conflict and violence prevention professionals working in highly traumatized communities who insist that community members retell their painful stories; leaders whose organizations compete for resources and recognition becoming rigid and competitive; environmental activists who refuse to listen to the wisdom of local indigenous peoples, make decisions that they believe to be the solution, yet eventually cause far more problems.

Through all that we witnessed and lived through, both of us learned that the pain of suffering can be transformed into compassion and altruism and shift dangerously chaotic situations into opportunities for healing, building resilience, and unification. We have also seen how, even in the most adverse conditions, people can reconcile their differences and rebuild healthy thriving communities. Those who cling to ideals of right and wrong often discover lasting, peaceful resolutions. We believe the world needs to nurture and cultivate kindness, compassion, and hope—and this can happen if everyone recognizes how our stories are interconnected and the merit of doing no harm.

As we began thinking about the social impact of 'harm', and our collective responsibility to 'do no harm', it became clear to us how early life experiences played a critical part in writing this book together. Although we were raised in two completely different places, (Thaïs, in the midst of the lush Santa Clara Valley in California, and Wendy, in the Mojave Desert along the Colorado River), we lived parallel lives.

The little desert town of 4,000 people was filled with interesting characters, good schools, a stable economy, a sense of place, a connection to a majestic river, and a love for the vast and empty spaces. Nestled next to the Mojave Indian Reservation, adding a rich diversity, it was by no means an environment of equity or inclusion. At the same time, it was hard to get lost. The town's people used to have a saying, "If you don't know who you are, just ask around. Someone else will be happy to tell you!" Everyone and everything was interconnected. Alongside the joy of being a kid, there were plenty of social and environmental challenges that one could not ignore. The heat was often unbearable, the flash floods wiped away landscapes and people in a heartbeat, and the winds ripped off roofs as if they were made of matchsticks. It was not uncommon to have young friends witness violence in their homes on a daily basis. Hunger and poverty were always present.

Growing up in a farm working community in Santa Clara Valley in California, there was a strong commitment to family and neighbors helping neighbors. Work meant picking fruit and nuts from the surrounding orchards and vineyards for the local canneries to process. Although money was scarce, and many of the children went to bed hungry, life had a quality of belonging to a place and to each other. As farm machinery manufacturers realized more money could be made making military machinery, middle class families moved to the valley to work for the new companies. This was the beginning of Silicon Valley. The small farming community began to be torn apart by a rise in violence, hatred, and destruction. White kid gangs pitted themselves against Mexican gangs, escalating conflict and creating the painful divide of haves and have nots. In a short decade, orchards and fertile farmland were bulldozed and replaced with asphalt for massive shopping centers, tract homes, and a tangle of highways broadcasting relentless noise. Multi-generational farmers lost their land while farm workers lost their jobs and were displaced into rundown neighborhoods. Domestic violence and child abuse increased, along with substance abuse and suicide.

In both places, there were no child protection or domestic violence services to be found. Churches could feed you, but only on Sunday. Why the violence? Why the inequity? Where was both safety and justice to be found? Where were the support systems? Where was the community when folks needed help? Could anyone help? And if so, who were they, and how would they be received? These were the questions haunting our childhoods which carried forward into our respective work as adults.

Navigating these experiences, and much more, was our practice, even as kids. We had no choice but to listen carefully but 'watch our mouth' and try to make sense of our experiences while at the same time trying to make sense of others' experiences. We had to learn to be resilient and develop strategies for swimming in treacherous waters, knowing we must "go as a river", as Zen Master Thich Nhat Hanh so eloquently states.

As both of us left our small communities and moved into the world, pursuing education, work, and creating our families, compassionate action and the desire to not harm others was central to our personal and professional lives. Years later, when we met in a doctoral program in Human Science and Transformative Social Change, we decided to work on a collaborative research project on the social importance of 'doing no harm'. We saw that our common experiences had shaped us as adults and was now influencing our academic work. This book has been inspired by our shared experiences.

MINDFUL ENGAGEMENT

By three methods we may learn wisdom:
first, by reflection, which is the noblest; second,
by imitation, which is easiest; and third by
experience, which is the bitterest.

—CONFUCIUS

The world is a perilous and complicated place, and the sheer magnitude of human suffering and environmental destruction is incomprehensible. While many of us dream of a kinder, more just, and safer world, we may also feel burdened by powerlessness and despair. How we respond in such times takes deliberate, conscious awareness. It requires us to show up as our best possible selves.

But how are we to do this? If we sit back and hope that things will improve, that will most likely never happen. We need the skills, ability, and willingness to work together towards a freer and better civil society. We must lead from both our hearts and our minds. We must learn how to act in ways that do not harm, from a place of balanced determination and with equal regard for all people—from a place of equanimity. This book is designed to help you do just that. The qualities, the stories and the practices within this book, provide the insight, skills, and tools needed to embrace our shared humanity, build resilience, transform conflict, and create meaningful change. This is a guide book that will give you the opportunity to understand and practice the principles and qualities of Mindful Engagement, as well as an opportunity to read stories of people whose lives and work represent these qualities.

The voices you will hear within this book include:

- A mediator whose work has redefined the field of mediation, conflict resolution, and peace building throughout the world;

- A Roman Catholic nun whose activism around issues of human rights, along with her public presence, has influenced national political and social decisions and policies;

- An indigenous grandmother and activist working tirelessly to save the birthing grounds of the caribou in Alaska from oil drilling;

- A woman who, along with her husband, creates a healing center for mothers and children living in Fukushima and suffering from radiation exposure;

- A pediatric psychiatrist and early childhood trauma expert who has reshaped our understanding and approach to working with children exposed to violence and neglect;

- A social worker who founded a job-training, earth-stewardship program for former inmates and at-risk youth;

- A mother who loses her son in the 9/11 attacks on the World Trade Center in New York City and subsequently co-founds an organization united to turn grief into actions for peace.

The people in these stories exemplify the essence of what it means to work in ways that do no harm. Their shared wisdom is a way finding—a way through. After years of experience, contemplation, successes, and failures, these people have embraced certain qualities they express as essential in their work and their daily lives—the qualities of Mindful Engagement. These core qualities that each person possesses, practices, embodies, and applies—authenticity, deep listening, wise speech, mindfulness, compassion, love and joy—are part of a wheel, an intersection of pain and beauty, where one informs the other.

Whether you are a social activist, educator, healthcare worker, community advocate, or someone who is wanting to 'just do something' to alter the course of the challenges we face as a society, engaging mindfully can become a source and foundation for bringing actions into the world that do not harm. Mindful engagement is a practice, and like all practices, the more we live it, the more we can fully embrace, embody, and share it with others. If we are to act for the common good while navigating ordinary, as well as difficult and perilous situations, then we must do so responsibly, with good intentions, confidence, purpose, and kindness. Our mindful presence, focused attention, and motivations will support the change we are hoping to initiate and realize.

HOW TO USE THE BOOK

This book offers practices that guide you, the reader, through a process to better understand the qualities of mindful engagement so that you can act with compassion and altruism, while contributing to the common good, avoiding divisiveness and polarization.

Practices take, well, *practice*. While we know that different people learn in different ways, we encourage you to read and use the practices in this book in increments, and not all at once. Take the time to consider each of the qualities of mindful engagement on its own. You may want to spend a full day, a week, or even longer, with each one. Give yourself the gift of time to explore the considerations, questions, and actions we suggest. You will probably think of more! Make the practices applicable to what you're doing every day. The practices may look different to a healthcare provider than they might to a preschool teacher or a community organizer.

You may find that journaling is a way to help you better understand your own experiences, bringing clarity and full attention to the practices of Mindful Engagement. A separate journal or bound notebook may be helpful for you to jot down your own notes.

THE PRACTICES OF MINDFUL ENGAGEMENT

- *Consider This* provides an opportunity for reflection related to the qualities. Spend time with them and do so with focused attention. This can be a starting point for you to bring clarity to your own thinking and intentions.

- *Now Ask Yourself* poses a series of questions that will help you gain insight and knowledge about your thought patterns, belief systems, and values, particularly as they relate to each quality and your own story.

- *Now Practice* is a way for you to engage with the qualities in a deliberate way. These guided practices include specific activities, observations, journaling, and paying attention 'on purpose' to your actions and the actions of others. Adapt the practice to your personal and professional circumstances as you see fit

- *Community of Practice* is an opportunity for you to practice the qualities with other people—informal groups of friends, colleagues, family—who are connected through shared experiences and interests. This part of the practice provides space for you to share knowledge, ideas, and experiences.

THE COMMON GOOD

If you've come here to help me, you're
wasting your time. But if you've come because
your liberation is bound up with mine,
then let us work together.

—LILLA WATSON

We are living in a world of increasing violence, pandemic level threats to our health, systemic racial injustice, devastation of our planet, and disconnection from our families and communities. Our hearts are breaking. There is a palpable climate of disconnect, violence, divisiveness, and neglect. There are wars on many fronts. We are at war with each other, with our neighbors, with our communities, with other nations. Global pandemics are taking lives and livelihoods from millions of people around the globe, while leaders wrestle how to effectively respond. The earth has lost half of its wildlife in the past forty years. Rapid climate change is contributing to devastating natural disasters. Children are killing children. It is difficult to envision any real alternative and so we may become both complicit and avoidant. We are becoming, quite rightly, overwhelmed with legitimate cause for fear and unrest that demands we take action as global environmental and social injustice threaten our very existence. Yet in the midst of all of this polarization, violence, and dis-ease, human beings have an innate desire to rectify wrong-doing and protect what we hold dear, with equanimity—equal consideration for all people and the world in which we live.

Many of us make a modest attempt to act in ways that don't harm others. We don't walk away from a friend who is going through hard times simply because we're in a bad mood, nor do we purposely throw trash in front of our neighbor's house. Rather than turn the other cheek and ignore injustice such as racism or xenophobia, we advocate and vote for equity and inclusion. And while we might disagree with someone who doesn't share our point of view, we refrain from verbally insulting and demeaning that person.

Most of us are familiar with that phrase, 'do no harm,' which comes from the Hippocratic oath, *primum non nocere*, or "first, do no harm." This fundamental global ideal requires that we minimize the harm that is inadvertently caused by our actions. It asks that we be aware of how the consequences of those actions may contribute to wide-ranging and complex repercussions which may be immediate or long term. Mahatma Gandhi rooted his philosophy in *ahimsa*, the overflowing love that arises when all ill will, anger, and hate have subsided from the heart. *Ahimsa* is accomplished by following the precepts of causing no injury through right action, including deeds, thoughts, and words. Gandhi believed *ahimsa* to be a creative force that could lead to one's divine truth and applied this principle and moral imperative of 'do no harm' to all living things.

We believe that the world is in need of a new kind of diplomacy and social sensibility, equipped with the motivation and tools to transform our heartfelt intentions into altruism—compassionate actions which support the common good. This is not just about the individual—we are in this together. Now is the time to cultivate our benevolent virtues, recognize our interconnectedness, and appeal to the best instincts of the human spirit. For our social world to exist with some degree of harmony, we cannot rely on others to make things better. Each one of us needs to step up in the best way possible and contribute to the changes we wish to see happen. A single interaction that is mindful and compassionate has the potential to bring a sense of hope and provide motivation to find solutions that may not otherwise have been discovered. If we can maintain an attitude of doing our best amidst the flux and confusion of daily life as well as the perilous time we're in today, we can come to realize that this is what many others are also trying to do.

There is a social and universal responsibility to act, for both enlightened self-interest as well as for the benefit of all. Society has within it both value and practice which are central to ideals of justice and human rights. Transcending gender, class, race, religion, and culture, compassion in action is focused on all humanity, giving us possibilities for global civility while upholding the virtues of human dignity. We must include regulating and rewarding interactions so that people do not feel marginalized, stressed, or become disengaged. When we neglect these responsibilities, harm occurs—harm that is potentially devastating if we fail to pay attention. We cannot go in and rip out parts of people's lives and expect them to remain whole.

So what are we to do? How might we reimagine the ways in which we engage as human beings on this precious planet? How can we best contribute to the health, safety and happiness of our friends and family, and all humanity? More simply put: What is required of us to live and work in ways that do not harm others or the planet? Answering this question can be a challenging, if not daunting, task, especially as more complex and difficult circumstances plague us.

Where do we begin? We can begin with examining our role

and responsibility for what's happening in our world. We can decide to become involved in making changes, whether it's at work, in our family, our neighborhood or some social or political action that can positively impact the challenges we face. We may decide to do something radically different, learn new ways of engaging and tools for forgiveness and reconciliation. And we are not alone in this journey. There are plenty of examples of people who we can turn to for inspiration.

Inspired by Martin Luther King, Jr., Congressman John Lewis left his home in rural Alabama, starting what would become a lifetime of social and political activism. Despite continued threats, intimidation, and brutal physical attacks, he maintained his commitment to nonviolence and equality for all people. As an astute observer with a fearless mission to end racial segregation in the South, John Lewis' journey was long and difficult, yet he persevered. He spoke to the values of faith, patience, study, truth, peace, love, and reconciliation. "Real leaders are not appointed," Lewis said. "They emerge out of the masses of the people and rise to the forefront through the circumstances of their lives. Either their inner journey or their human experience prepares them to take that role. They do not nominate themselves. They are called into service by a spirit moving through a people that points to them as the embodiment of the cause they serve."

The idea of collective social responsibility is at the root of a healthy society. Traditional teachings of many indigenous peoples refer to responsibility as much more than taking matters into one's own hands. When solving a problem or settling a dispute, for example, they focus on much more than a single aspect of someone's existence. Attention is paid, with respect, to all things that influence a person's life—community, family, the environment, ancestors, and spirit.

For native Hawai'ians, *kuleana* is a deeply held notion that there is value in responsibility that transcends rights, interests, privileges, and ownership. There is honor and gratitude when one takes responsibility. Kuleana is something one possesses and extends far beyond our personal and professional lives, reaching deep into the physical, spiritual, and ancestral worlds. There is no ignoring your kuleana and the clarity and honesty it brings. It is to be shared. And when practiced, kuleana brings about transformation and one becomes *ho'ohiki*—keeping the promises you make to yourself and others. Once you have kept those promises, you can stand behind your convictions, your ways of knowing, your belief systems, and be accountable in all respects—not simply for the task at hand, but the entire world in which you live.

Ubuntu is an African word for human kindness. It is the belief in a universal bond of sharing that connects all of humanity. The virtue of ubuntu asserts that being part of "the tribe," or society, gives humans their humanity. We can't exist in isolation, and when you possess ubuntu, you are warm and generous. "We are because you are," and "I am" because "you are." Ubuntu is both a deep appreciation of individual uniqueness and collective social responsibility. For South Africans, they owe this quality of interconnectedness to each other. Aboriginal Australians share a deeply held belief of *kanyini*, or responsibility—a responsibility that applies to one's belief systems, spirituality, family, and land. There is no separating them. If you take a piece out of one, the others will falter. They are intricately linked in this web of responsibility.

So it is when we are doing our work in the world. We must be mindful of our kanyini, our ubuntu, our kuleana, our responsibility that is carried from our past into our present if we are to

engage in ways that do not harm. Doing our part in a community that intentionally encourages collective responsibility and
a genuine sense of belonging can be a source of strength and
purpose. For meaningful change to happen we must take on the
tasks together. When we do this, our authentic self emerges,
giving us the freedom to act mindfully and compassionately
with the hope that anything is possible. We are being asked to
come together, not for self-interest, but for the benefits we gain
through cooperation and a willingness to make a contribution
to the well-being of humanity. The awakening of an open, kind,
and good heart helps us find the way toward right actions with
the purest of motivations for the good of others and ourselves.

It takes courage to step out of what feels comfortable, what we
think is true, and give ourselves permission to make choices
which better align with our values and altruistic nature. We
can think of and act in new ways to work with communities
that constrain us and within systems that bind us. "If we are a
drop of water and we try to get to the ocean as only an individual drop, we will surely evaporate along the way," says Thich
Nhat Hanh. "To arrive at the ocean, you must go as a river. The
sangha (community) is your river. Allow your community to
hold you, to transport you," he says. "When you do, you will
feel more solid and stable and will not risk drowning in your
suffering. As a river, all the individual drops of water arrive
together at the ocean."

The capacity to reach out and find ways of transforming our
knowledge into action, is one of the keys to guiding us toward
possible solutions. We must find ways to develop equanimity
and engage mindfully and do so without causing harm in a
way that unifies rather than creates polarization. This type of
engagement is not a formula or structured way of doing work—

one that compartmentalizes our thinking, establishes protocols, creates models, and introduces methodologies. Nor is this way of engaging asking us to abide by some kind of plan or approved way of acting, or to fixate on some ideal of how we are supposed to be. Rather, Mindful Engagement is a guide to assist us in cultivating and utilizing inherent qualities and live our lives in a way that translates into meaningful, effective, and rewarding experiences for ourselves and others. Living and working in this way has the potential of making situations better, while deepening our understanding of others'—and our own—perspectives and experiences.

As the practices and the stories in this book remind us, practicing mindfulness, learning to be more compassionate, using our words wisely, listening deeply, being authentic, embracing the ideals of equity, working for the common good, and doing so with love and joy, are essential tools if we are to meet the unique social and environmental challenges of our time. Through mindful engagement, we may well discover more qualities, more approaches, and more practices that suit the times we live in.

THE QUALITIES STORIES AND PRACTICES OF MINDFUL ENGAGEMENT

THE QUALITY OF AUTHENTICITY
KNOW YOURSELF

I wish that every life be
pure transparent freedom.

—SIMONE DE BEAUVOIR

*A*uthenticity is at the heart of a person's presence, along with the conviction and confidence to stay true to themselves. Being an authentic human being brings in wisdom and clarity, and keeps us more grounded in reality. Our true nature and compassionate heart is discovered and honored.

Nosce te ipsum: Know yourself. This inquiry into our true nature is at the heart of understanding what it means to be an authentic human being. While this may be hard, and even frightening, it is worth the effort. In whatever work we do and however we choose to live our lives, it is essential that we know ourselves so that we can create opportunities to act independently, with grace and compassion. We can then give ourselves permission to make free choices within our economic, political, emotional, spiritual, and social spaces. This is what it means to be an authentic human being. When we are in the presence of authentic people who are attuned and selfless, there is a unique quality about them. Their lives seem to flow in meaningful and rewarding ways. Faced with difficulties, these people engage in ways that support mutually acceptable and responsible solutions. They are not immune to the emotional and physical challenges of everyday life, and yet their presence has a certain confidence, wisdom, grace, and calm.

Each one of us carries our own wisdom and authenticity which is woven into our motivations, intentions, and responses to individual and collective experiences. When we are our authentic selves, we have a strong sense of the value of moving through our lives in ways that provide flexibility, freedom, and autonomy. It is not necessary for us to work in isolation, or on our own, or without the participation and contribution of others. If we are true to ourselves, we are free to become more curious and explore possibilities, and permit ourselves to more easily collaborate and engage with other people. We are able to break down barriers which can lead toward meaningful and lasting solutions to the problems and challenges we encounter.

When we are being authentic, we are not afraid to step outside of what society deems possible. And while finding ourselves in totally new territory and without customary support systems (which can be scary and uncertain), authentic people choose to exercise their agency and can exert our power or influence, without causing harm. There is a freedom to act, a liberation of sorts, from the constraints that may bind us from doing our best work and living our lives with courage, meaning and purpose. Powerful and energizing, when we are able to see the quality of authenticity in ourselves and in others, we are given a grounded sense of hope that anything is possible.

In today's world, people's dignity and worth are under assault, yet we must not lose sight of our uniqueness and value as individuals and as communities. There is solidarity and commitment around what we believe to be most important, while at the same time valuing the potential contributions from all sources available to us. When we work from this place of authenticity, there is a sense of openness and liberation. Being aware of our authentic self becomes an opportunity to share possibilities and open doors for new ways of thinking and working.

In a teaching from the Buddha, there is a story that reflects the rarity of our humanness. "Monks," said the Buddha, "suppose that this great earth was totally covered with water and a man were to toss a yoke with a single hole there. A wind from the east would push it west, a wind from the west would push it east. A wind from the north would push it south, a wind from the south would push it north. And suppose a blind sea turtle was there. It would come to the surface once every one hundred years. Now what do you think? Would that blind sea turtle, coming to the surface once every one hundred years, stick his neck into the yoke with a single hole?" "It would be a sheer coincidence, lord," said the monks, "that the blind sea turtle, coming to the surface once every one hundred years, would stick his neck into the yoke with a single hole." The Buddha replied, "It's likewise a sheer coincidence that one obtains the human state."

Our authentic self cannot be realized by simply repeating a set of actions, taking up a set of positions, or trusting our familiar patterns of thoughts and behaviors. It is vital we remain true to our own spirit and character in times of rapid change and uncertainty. We must take the time to surface, not every one hundred years as the blind sea turtle, but every day if we are to find our way. Our work, our lives, our relationships, our actions, are rooted in this basic sense of commitment—a devotion to the things we hold most dear.

STORIES THAT MATTER

Kenneth Cloke, JD, PhD
Bruce D. Perry, MD, PhD
Joan Goldsmith, PhD

KENNETH CLOKE, JD, PHD

Exploring ways to resolve complex interpersonal, organizational, and social problems in ways that have lasting effects for the greater good is by no means an easy task. Yet Kenneth Cloke has transformed the thinking around dialogue, mediation, and peacemaking. He offers us insight into the delicate nature of working in difficult, and often quite challenging, environments, while at the same time, stressing the importance of the embodied nature and practice of meaningful engagement.

"The highest expression of our values is to become the thing that we believe in."

Engagement with others is engagement with the self. If you try to have one without the other, you will be limited and unable to reach the highest levels. So we can simply see each as the limit of the other, as in calculus, where we get closer and closer to the fullest expression of one, and immediately begin to slip into the other. If we go far enough north on a sphere, we will begin to head south. Conflict is all about self and other. The heart-based, empathetic values of conflict resolution and altruistic caring for one another are mistakenly understood as things that can be added on in mediation, but they are actually the ground of the conflict-resolution experience and of self-actualization. What we are missing in our conflict conversations is that it takes us to the ground of our experience, and when we are in a place of love, we are grounded in that moment and are able to manifest our most basic, authentic, best selves.

I became deeply involved in efforts to expand freedom and equality during the 1960s, and was active in the Free Speech Movement at the University of California, Berkeley in 1960. But it was not until I went to work in the South, in the Civil Rights Movement, that I began to realize what real social engagement meant, and understood that I was not simply doing this for others, but so that I could have a better life. Doing community organizing as a university student in Berkeley was one thing, but it was quite another in Alabama and South Georgia. The idea that we should do no harm needs to acknowledge that in trying to reduce the level of harm, it is sometimes necessary to stand and be counted.

I remember the first moment this idea occurred to me. When I was an undergraduate at the Berkeley campus, ROTC was compulsory. A young man I knew refused to participate. This was complicated by the fact that his father was a career military officer, and he was going to be expelled for his refusal. Yet he began a fast in front of the Administration Building and asked people to sign a petition against compulsory ROTC. Coming out of the McCarthy era, you didn't sign petitions because it could destroy your entire career and possibly your life. I had to struggle with myself as I decided to sign the petition. For me, this was not simply social engagement, but internal self-engagement, and a direct, profound realization that whatever happens to other people also happens to you. This wasn't entirely about this young man or other people. It was also about me. There are many ways of denying this interconnectedness and distancing ourselves from it, but the fundamental fact is "it's all ours." Ultimately, there are no "Them" and "Us"—there's just us.

When I worked in the South, in the Civil Rights Movement, with tenant farmers who, in my opinion, had far more wisdom than

I did, it became clear to me that it was not completely accurate to describe this as something we were doing for other people, or to say that we were courageous. It was something we were doing for all of us, and we benefitted as much as the people we work with. While it is true that doing so took courage, it is also true that together with courage came freedom of thought and of soul—freedom to step outside of received wisdom and look back and make our own choices, and that's quite extraordinary. At times we had to ask ourselves, "Am I willing to give my life for this? Does this matter enough to give my life?" But it was through that very act of giving that we gained our lives. We are all deeply, essentially social in our nature. John Donne was right when he said, "Therefore, never send to know for whom the bell tolls, it tolls for thee." This interconnectedness is what is lost in conflict, and can be regained in mediation.

There are a number of definitions of enlightenment in Buddhism. One of the ones I like best is "being available for anything at any moment." To me, this means not being stuck. It is possible to become attached to our own suffering and not want to escape it. Whatever we can't see inside ourselves becomes a blind spot that keeps us from seeing that same thing in others. We simply miss it. It's important to look deeply into our selves in order to see what is true in the world. We are not isolated from the rest of the world. We are in this together. With this kind of thinking comes a need for empathy and compassion. Empathy and compassion are valuable sources of information about what is happening to another person that help eliminate the blind spots within ourselves. Using them, we can voluntarily place ourselves, through the mechanism of suffering, in the circumstances of the other, and know our own suffering. Wherever there is suffering, that suffering is also ours. If it harms me, it harms you.

The words we use are critical and we need to practice empathetic and compassionate forms of communication that do not create the illusion of separation. At the same time, words must not aggravate the wounds of others. While each of us experiences conflict well below the level of language, for the most part we recount, mediate, and resolve them using language. As a result, words can never suffice to describe what or how we feel when we are in conflict. Yet they also form an essential part of the process when we are trying to resolve conflict. For example, certain words do not have the same meaning to women as they do to men. What does the word "wife" mean? It will predictably mean something different to a man than a woman, as will the word "husband" and the word "marriage" to pick just three. From a very early age, the meaning of these words is socially reinforced and overlaid with a lifetime of experiences.

The German sociologist, Theodor Adorno, wrote in *The Jargon of Authenticity* that there is a way of communicating about things that makes them less authentic. Social entities perform a kind of social hypnosis. Things are talked about in ways that convince us that they exist when in reality, they don't. They become figments of our imaginations. Within these entities, where there is authenticity, there is the courage and willingness to step outside of what society describes as possible—what our own minds tell us is possible. Individually, this is connected not only to critical thinking, but also to mindfulness in that it has a quality of being stripped of illusions, expectations, and whatever it is we think belongs to us. Until we have been stripped in that way, we don't have a sense of who we are in the absence of pretense, illusion, and a socially constructed framework. We have to take ourselves outside that framework and accept a kind of exile. Only in this way does freedom become real.

In the process, humility also becomes important as we realize that we are not perfect. Moreover, mediation is not an equal relationship with the parties, because the mediator is outside the problem, yet in order to mediate we need to recognize we are no different from the parties but are capable of engaging in all their worst behaviors. To succeed, I have to find the people I am working with inside of me, and allow myself to experience their conflict directly, while at the same time remaining outside of it. As a mediator, I can do something from the outside that can't be done from the inside, and vice versa.

When we are acting in ways that we think may serve some greater good, it is possible to become a kind of moral imperialism and impose our values on others. All we have to do to cause harm—serious harm—is to believe sincerely that we are right and others are wrong. What flows from this conviction is the justification of force and violence. Many I knew have slipped on that path. It is also possible to lose our way in moral relativism, which requires only that we sincerely believe that anything and everything is morally acceptable. The difficulty is how we thread our way through the maze created by these two sets of beliefs. The highest expression of our values is to become the thing that we believe in. Our work then becomes an expression of who and what we are. Until then, we are imperfect in realizing our values, which is what makes it a value.

To choose to value love and become a more loving person is a beautiful choice and one that feels absolutely right for mediators. Yet in our line of work, this is not a small thing and it often takes courage to act in loving ways toward others. At this moment, right now, if we do not act, we may lose a unique opportunity. Consider Rosa Parks going to the front of the bus. The time was right, and she felt it along with many others who were thinking, "If we don't stand up now, we lose." In those moments, her strength shifted and these turning points became a true force in the movement for social change. It is this ability to glimpse the human soul of the other that flows from love and yet informs all of our work.

Engagement with others, for me, is therefore a deep act of love in which I do my best to dismantle my own defenses and delight in knowing the other, and in the process, arrive at some higher order, value-based, synergistic understanding. It is a kind of freedom, yet it is also a kind of exile from the hypnosis and fetishism engendered by simplistic social constructs. Engagement and love then becomes a way of connecting with the unique human beings who are in front of me. To feel and know when someone or something is broken, and then do something together to fix it—that is love ... that is deep love.

BRUCE D. PERRY, MD, PHD

Engaging with traumatized individuals, groups, and systems is complex. As a clinician, researcher, and author in the field of childhood trauma and social and health systems reform, Dr. Bruce Perry shares his thinking about the value of understanding the neurobiology of relationships and the importance of those who work in demanding environments to enter into these experiences, as well as these systems, in ways that are well attuned and relational in nature.

"Hope is basically an internal representation that there can be a better outcome."

During the Waco, Texas FBI siege of David Koresh's Branch Davidian compound, I was brought in as a child psychiatrist to help with the children who had been living there, and who had been released into State custody in the first three days following the initial ATF raid. These children were clearly traumatized. This group of children had a completely different belief set than most of the people working with them—beliefs about what's right, what's wrong, the way the world worked. In the beginning, they actually thought we were going to kill them. I think one of the most important things I learned from that experience was that being parallel and being a presence, not engaging face to face or as an inquisitor, ended up being very powerful. As an example, these children had different beliefs about what you could eat and how you could eat it—all made up by David Koresh. In the compound, they were forced to comply with his directives: he decided when, what, and how much everyone would eat. The children had no opportunity to make choices. The restrictions and prohibitions about food and choice were deeply ingrained in these children. So when they first came in, we didn't try to change this. We let the children continue with their dietary beliefs, but we let the staff around them eat what they (as staff) would normally eat. We were with these children all day long for weeks and ate every meal with them, so the kids could see the difference. Ultimately, the children asked for bites of what was otherwise prohibited, abandoned some of the absurd dietary prohibitions, and began eating in a more typical way. We did this with other things like behaviors around sleep, dress, and religious beliefs. They were able to see alternatives that were in a respectful and safe environment so they could make their own choices. Giving them opportunities to observe, explore, and try on new ways, they slowly built the confidence and comfort to leave their comfort zone, and move to what we felt were healthier more developmentally appropriate choices around behavior and belief.

What are the elements that make an interaction regulating and rewarding versus an interaction that makes people feel distressed, disengaged, or marginalized? It's something I think about quite a bit. We now live in an increasing sensory over-stimulated environment where good people who would otherwise be capable of relating in very positive ways are continually pulled away from meaningful engagement. Things that keep us away from being present in a relational way.

The ability of someone to be present in a respectful way during human interactions is absolutely at the heart of regulating neurobiology capable during a relational interaction. This is the way human beings are capable of making other human beings feel safe, feel pleasure, feel understood. It's something I think we need to learn how to do better. We need to have some discipline about how we create environmental circumstances that facilitate the capacity to remain present, attuned, and responsive in these good ways. All kinds of things can interfere with that unfortunately quite fragile state of being fully present. I know that with practice, however, people can get better at becoming more present and attuned.

At the core, human beings are really relational creatures. We have these neurobiological preferences for working and living and playing in groups. We are inclined to be in organizations. The way our brain is organized, at least with regards to relational neurobiology, is to some degree a reflection of these environments. When we run into people who are from our primary groups and are safe and familiar, we feel regulated. If we run into people who are different from our groups—in other words, we don't know them—the default response is to activate our threat response and view them as a potential threat. This double-edge sword in our neurobiology of relationships plays a big role in a tremendous number of problems like racism, nationalism, misogyny, and all sorts of other "isms." There are a variety of interpersonal strategies that are adaptive and healthy and a number that are adaptive and unhealthy. Some may be adaptive in your family, but you go into another family or organization and these strategies are maladaptive. We're trying to understand the complexity of these dynamic relational situations. Think about the number of possible interactions and groupings that can take place with a group of just eight people: it's around 1,250 interactions. When you are in an organization with five hundred people this number gets enormous. There is a tremendous complexity to it, but at its core the fundamental ability to establish relationships is formed from these developmental experiences and sets of associations that we create fairly early in life.

People use language as much to conceal as they do to reveal. A lot of our work ends up being much more about nonverbal communication and different forms of somatosensory inter- action. The rhythm and tone of language is quite important. Sometimes if the tone of voice carries the emotional intention of the communicator, even the wrong words don't hurt or have the same negative impact. This nonverbal vehicle can make people feel okay without the words. We see this a lot with peo- ple "saying the right thing" but the effect that's underneath it is hollow. That's as much a harmful act as the words you say.

We've done a similar thing in our work with very radicalized Muslim kids who are raised in an environment where they are taught to hate Westerners—basically raised as jihadists. What do you do? Do you prohibit them being around it? The answer is no. You find an appropriate moderate Muslim religious leader who will be present in their lives, allowing them to see the ways to be respectful of their fundamental religious beliefs, but no longer reinforce the marginal elements of that indoc- trinated belief system. Eventually, their radical belief systems can dissolve away.

Another long, complex, larger-scale situation was when we were asked to work with the children and mothers of the Fundamen- talist Church of Latter-day Saints in Utah associated with their leader, Warren Jeffs. He was arrested and prosecuted for his arrangement of illegal marriages between adult male followers and underage girls. Many of the individuals, including the wives, were given opportunities to engage with other Mormons who did not have abnormal variants of the Mormon belief system.

They stepped away from that manipulated and exploited version of their faith toward the mainstream set of beliefs.

Human beings have this very powerful desire to connect. If you create a situation, clinically or otherwise, where you are in their presence long enough, they can't resist the very powerful neurobiological pull to be connected. As long as you don't push or impose your beliefs on them and give them an opportunity to see that you are safe and consistent and predictable and nurturing, ultimately you can create lines of communication that would not be possible in other circumstances.

We talk a lot about issues of inequality. If you work with children, there is a fundamental power differential that is created between the large adult and the smaller child. If you are a mental health professional, it's even magnified. This inequality and imbalance is inevitable. In our work, we talk about the fact that the power differential can shift. As much as possible, our staff provides the people we work with an opportunity to minimize this power differential. We try to do the work in the home or community where they are at the top of a power differential, rather than the clinician being at the top. The more equal starting point in the therapeutic process facilitates the creation of respectful, effective, and collaborative helping relationships. We also try to be explicit in helping them understand some fundamental rhythms to the ways healthy relationships function.

Hope is a big part of our work. I think it's a quality that we can embrace and is tremendously powerful. If you are with an individual, you are fully engaged and they feel that you really do care, they internalize that. They can store it and use it again and again and again. They will have stored that human connection that can be real. It can be honest. It can feel safe. It can give pleasure. And even if right now they experience relational poverty, loneliness, and marginalization, they can use the memory of the previous true connected moment(s) to feel a sense of hope. What we do know is that one interaction has the potential to literally create and shape a sense of hope for a child, as an example that will keep them motivated, engaged, and working toward healthier goals than they might have otherwise done.

Sadly, a lot of these children, youth, and adults just quit. Some of the best evidence of this is that we spend literally hundreds of thousands of dollars on many of these children, but their outcomes are terrible. Part of it is because a lot of the people who work with these children and families have difficulty controlling their emotions, so overwhelmed, that they can't be fully present and engaged. In turn, if you talk to some of these kids after they've grown out of the system and you asked them, "What really helped?" they frequently describe a single contact with one person who truly made a difference in their life. I recall one child who was doing quite well, after having experienced twenty-seven foster care placements within the course of thirty days, tell me how important one person in particular was for helping them feel safe.

So you have to do something else. I would say that the best evidence for what is therapeutic has been collected over centuries in dozens of independent countries and most of the continents. All of them converge on the fact that "what is therapeutic?" is this: relationally rich, patterned, repetitive, rhythmic somatosensory activity... period. These patterned neural activations are necessary for children to self-regulate—things like having predictable nurturing caregivers, relational stability, music, movement, yoga, drumming, art. It's the most powerful evidence you can find. The independent convergence on these concepts, across multiple cultures all over the planet, is the most powerful form of "evidence" that exists. One of the elegant things about biological systems is that simple, unifying principles are usually much more powerful and accurate than convoluted, disconnected, and seemingly independent processes and explanations. There's a synchrony and coherence to the organization of complex systems, and if you really understand this, you're not surprised at all by the convergence and wisdom of the core elements of healing from indigenous healing practices.

JOAN GOLDSMITH, PHD

Experiences matter, and Joan Goldsmith is able to tell
her stories in a way that gives clarity to the formation
and development of an activist. Growing up during the
McCarthy era and coming of age in the 1960's, Joan speaks
to the environments and the people who helped shape her
thinking and resulting actions with respect to peace, conflict
resolution, education reform, civil rights, and leadership. Her
honesty and transparency bring light to the evolution of the
self and why it matters that we act for the common good.

"Meaningful engagement requires
that we notice, pay attention in a different
way, and see who we really are."

I think the family of my birth first influenced my social
engagement. My dad was a labor organizer. When he had
been fired from *The New York Times* in 1936, for organizing a
union, and was not reinstated in his job by a National Labor
Relations Board hearing, he took a job with John L. Lewis as
an organizer for the CIO, the radical conglomerate of workers
that represented the mine workers, steel workers, and the
autoworkers. He was given a war deferment during World War
II to support the Longshoremen's union in keeping the New Jer-
sey shipyard open to maintain the war effort.

I grew up in an environment of social activism. I would sit on
street corners with my mother, who was giving out leaflets with
political messages. I was active as a child and remember sitting

on my Dad's shoulders as we marched in Labor Day parades. We worked a lot for racial integration, and I remember when Paul Robeson, the black opera singer, actor, and scholar came to our home and lifted me up with that very deep voice saying, "So this is little Joan."

I was raised in an environment of Left politics by both parents. When the McCarthy era began and the Rosenbergs were tried and convicted of spying and killed, I was frightened. We moved to Louisville, Kentucky because this was the only community my parents felt safe. The House Security Commission subpoenaed my dad when the Rosenbergs were being killed. His testimony was all over the press. He didn't give them anything they didn't already have. My mom was fired from her job as a secretary when my father was in the press, and my friends in the Jewish community told me that their parents didn't want them going to my house, because, "If the FBI finds out, you won't get into college." I was only thirteen years old. As a result, I became an advocate for civil rights and at fourteen years old, I invited black and white kids to meet together in the Louisville Jewish Community Center.

In college I became a fervent activist, joining committees and demonstrating. In graduate school, I worked in Robert Taylor Homes housing project, where Obama worked nineteen years after me. I organized the parents to create a parent-led preschool and worked in black communities to create Freedom Schools between 1964-66. I was clear that I did not want to pay the price my parents paid when they gave up their lives as activists. I knew I wanted to have a life: an identity separate from the movement. This was a huge decision for me and is still with me when I think about social engagement. To this day, I will not lose myself in work.

The turning point in my understanding of how to work in ways that do no harm was in 1968, when I began teaching at South Boston High School. It was ultimately the National Guard that forced the integration of the school at gunpoint in 1974. Teachers would let white students abuse African American students. White kids were known to dangle black kids out the school windows by their feet. It was an Irish enclave—poor Irish—and they were protecting what they had. I chose to go there, not to any other school, as a teacher and an activist, hoping to end racism on campus. I prepared elegant lessons, activities, and speeches that I was going to give while teaching American History. I used all the Left literature, and had brilliant lesson plans.

I went into the classroom and discovered that these lessons didn't mean a thing to my students. What I thought had nothing to do with connecting with what was important to these students. I invited kids from the school to go with me on Saturdays to see where the American Revolution was fought on the Boston Common. I arranged to have groups of African American students with whom I worked come and share their music with the students from South Boston and vice versa. As the kids got to know each other and were friendly, the parents started to attack me for being a Communist. The parents also criticized me because I taught current events in my American History classes every Friday, and yet the principal of the school defended me. I looked to myself to see where I was getting in the way, where I was suffering, and how the students—each of them in different ways—were suffering. This changed everything. I let go of my constructs, my "bringing" ideas and what they "should" know, and we focused on what was going on in their lives and how they could connect with each other. Not giving up who I am made for meaningful engagement with my students.

Meaningful engagement requires that we notice, pay attention in a different way, and see who we really are so that we bring our authentic self to our work. It is also important to use language that has not been corrupted. I have always been concerned when people become attached to an ideology. It may not be a political ideology. It can be when they declare, "I'm a Freudian; I'm a Jungian; I'm a member of...." It can become oppressive when ideologies clash and destroy projects. We must not lean into these rigid places but remain fluid, flexible, and transparent.

THE PRACTICE OF AUTHENTICITY

CONSIDER THIS

▶ Honor your worldview while leaving room for understanding and honoring other people's experiences and wisdom.

▶ Pay close attention to your own story as it is essential to understanding what has influenced your heart and your actions.

▶ Give yourself permission to make choices free from the constraints of friends, family, community and the society in which you live—constraints that may limit your ability to act with kindness, goodwill, and a social sensibility.

▶ And remember, in order to be authentic, you need to be willing to step outside of what society says is possible and act on what is true for you, without causing harm.

NOW ASK YOURSELF

▶ What does it mean for me to live an authentic life?

- Am I able to stay true to convictions, ethics, and myself?

- If yes, how do I go about doing so?

- If not, then why not?

- Do I feel free to act and think independently, with some degree of confidence in myself and the result of my actions?

▶ Do I hold onto long standing positions that might interfere with my ability to change my mind, when necessary?

- Are there obstacles I face if I were to re-evaluate those positions?

- If so, what are those obstacles?

- Do I find myself repeating actions or taking positions that no longer serve me or others?

- Am I willing to step outside what I thought was possible and imagine another outcome?

▶ Are there qualities within myself that I need to nurture so that I can live a more authentic life, putting my best and authentic self forward? Qualities such as:

- Independence

- Flexibility

- Hopefulness

- Openness

- Willingness

NOW PRACTICE

▶ Making Sense of Your Stories

- Compose a one-page story of your origin—your roots, ancestry, family, community and country.

- Notice how that story plays into your behaviors and relationships, especially in situations that are related to issues of that impact society and the environment

- Now, compose a one-page story of who you think you are today—your relationships, work, likes and dislikes, values, and beliefs.

- Go back to these stories over time and see if they still hold true, or if there is more that needs to be said.

▶ Becoming More Authentic

- Think of 5 people who you consider to be authentic; either people you know or those who you have heard or read about. Jot down their names.

- What is it about these people that you find to be authentic?

- What stands out for you about their stories, thinking, emotions, behaviors... or something else?

- Find time to research and read about people who you consider to be authentic, compassionate, mindful, and generally happy and impactful people.

▶ Creating a Community of Practice

- Set some time aside with friends, family, or colleagues for a discussion that focuses on a subject of mutual interest related to social or political issues. (We suggest you start with social issues and move, gently, into political ones!)

- Bring your attention to the quality of authenticity before you begin.

- Ask the group how they think authenticity can contribute to living and working in ways that do not harm.

THE QUALITY OF WISE SPEECH AND DEEP LISTENING
SKILLFUL COMMUNICATION

Without words, without writing and
without books there would be no history,
there would be no concept of humanity.

—HERMANN HESSE

*L*istening *deeply and using words wisely*, both written and spoken, are foundational elements of skillful communication. We need to understand the value of building our skills if we are to engage mindfully and in ways that do no harm. Communication that is both skillful and compassionate builds relationships and requires wholehearted patience, attention, and presence in order to recognize the value of someone else.

The need for openness and understanding is becoming more urgent across the globe. We can choose to hold on to old ways of thinking and be bound by limited perspectives, or we can choose to be open and receptive, welcoming ideas and solutions in a rapidly changing world. This is not necessarily easy, especially in cultures where instant gratification and the urgency to get things done drives most daily activities. We must slow down and give ourselves time to connect with each other. These connections and bonds will sustain us through our efforts to build consensus toward the change we want to see in the world.

When we listen respectfully to others who have different opinions and life experiences than our own, we take the first step in accepting that there are a host of perspectives and points of view on issues. If we want real change, we need to have conversations that may be controversial and present some difficult moments. We needn't concede those points that define our values but rather, find ways to work together towards positive change that reflects our shared values. Jane Goodall, English primatologist and animal rights activist suggests, "What makes us human, I think, is an ability to ask questions, a consequence of our sophisticated spoken language. Change happens by listening and then starting a dialogue with the people who are doing something you don't believe is right." If we are willing to explore points of view through an exchange with others and explore what we share in common, we may find it supports the collaborative effort we need for the change we want to make.

The Quaker spiritual community emphasizes the value of deep listening by intentionally incorporating collective silence into gatherings. This process allows for time to contemplate what has been said and builds a sense of collective inquiry. Listening with attention, and not lapsing into discussion, is a necessary step to help suspend individual judgments and assumptions. This form of listening enriches the flow of exchanges and ideas as well as increasing trust between individuals and within the group.

Connecting with another through words and listening creates reciprocity—the responsive actions that allow us to fully participate in the act of giving and receiving. It is through this dialogue which provides us opportunities to explore shared ideas and values which strengthens our resolve to take action not just alone, but together. We must be prepared to move our own story out of the way, speaking truth to power and checking our own privilege and the blind spots it creates. It may feel awkward and uncomfortable at times to leave the familiar territory of sticking with our story or our set thinking of what we believe is true. This requires us to use words that are authentic and respectful, and listening in a way that allows us to change our mind—an opportunity for us to see the intersection and commonality of our shared ideas, values and desires.

Cultivating skillful communication can help us find a deeper connection and a greater ease with those we engage with, whether it be resolving conflicts, sharing stories and ideas or finding solutions to problems. Words resonate, for better or worse. As we hear words of sorrow, we may become disheartened. Worldviews are shaped by the words we hear and read. "Without words, without writing and without books, there would be no history, there would be no concept of humanity," writes Hermann Hesse. In order to find common ground and sustain a healthy society dedicated to stewardship and responsibility, we must choose our words wisely.

When we integrate wise speech into our communication skills, we begin to remove differences, inequalities, and misunderstandings. Words may become less threatening, less harmful, and we may feel more aligned with and a part of the community. When speaking in ways that do no harm, our words, and the ways we choose to use them, can support a natural unfolding of what is before us, giving people an opportunity to bring their voices forward and share their gifts of connections, understanding, and wisdom.

Language is an art form, and as such, requires skill. The diversity found within human language and expression is enough to make us pause before we speak—especially in new situations and unfamiliar places. Words hold power that can be used to instigate or neutralize any given experience. They can be used as weapons—either offense or defense. As we listen to stories of sorrow, we may become disheartened. As we listen to stories of hope, we may become hopeful. As we hear language that we consider to be full of racism and hatred, we may become angry or fearful. We need to be aware of the energy that our words hold and use them for the greater good, even in times that invoke fear and outrage. In order to do this, we must take into consideration the words *we* speak and how *we* listen, remembering the power of what we say and how we say it.

One of the keys to using language which can assist with the practice of mindful engagement is 'right speech', a term that has been used in ancient Indian and Buddhist texts, as well as in contemporary explorations and theories of communication. Within this practice, it is critical to choose words that express ourselves and our ideas in a way that reduces harm to others. We need to remember the consequences associated with our thoughts, for these thoughts are the fundamental platform for our words and actions. Violent speech, including abrasive and hateful words, creates violence. Kind words create kindness. Words that originate from the heart, from a place of peace and harmony, create peace and harmony. Every word is seen as shaping thoughts and actions, supporting views and outcomes. Using right speech helps us become aware of our thoughts so we can say what we mean and soften and even change the message for the better. Blurting something out, even if we see it as honesty and truth can be harsh. Your truth is not always my truth. We can find ways to use words that convey calmness and kindness. This is right speech—words that are filled with praise, and openness to new ways of thinking and acting.

Words in one culture may not even exist in another culture. We travel to a foreign land, hoping to bring healing and reconciliation to a given situation. We ask how someone might feel about what has happened, yet they have no words in their vocabulary for the word 'feeling,' nor do they express feelings in the same way. The way we use our words can also make for an uneven playing field, giving power to one person or group over another, which leads to the loss of fair and honest representation.

Too often language, even if it is well-meaning, assumes the same norm for everyone, which sets up a construct that anyone else is an 'other'. It is important that we use words that are sincere and respectful, realizing that harsh words, for example, can make others feel vulnerable. Our words should not be intended to set the other up for failure or disappointment. Consequently, we must refrain from using words that suggest we can predict what the other person will say or do. Curiosity, without judgment, is essential. Asking questions in ways that do not have hidden meanings but are honest, clear, and simple, will assist us with seeking clarity and understanding. If we use our words consciously and sincerely, we have the opportunity to bring forth new ideas, new information, and new ways of thinking.

The complement to wise speech is deep listening—paying attention to more than just words. It is listening through awareness of our thoughts, physical sensations, and emotions. With deep listening, there is a keen observation of the person who is talking, while noticing the sound of their voice, their facial expressions, the rhythm in which they are speaking, and the gestures they are using. It is listening for the story behind the story you are hearing. This is an essential form of awareness which requires not only practice and skill, but also a way of being present and fully engaged. It is a resource that can give us more insight as to who is in the room and what they are feeling and thinking. Deep listening includes physical awareness, cognitive reflection, and emotional attunement, giving us the ability to listen closely to subtleties, to the possibilities at hand, and to what is being said and what is not being said.

The body listens to the mind and the mind listens to the body. Paying attention to body sensations is a key element to deep listening and one that we need to remember. A knot in our stomach, a quickening of the heart, and sweat on the brow—these are signals which remind us to listen to our bodies along with the words that are being spoken. At any given moment, we can bring our attention back to the sensation of the body. As we listen, we may notice that our physical sensations may shift. This moment-to-moment awareness attunes us to responses in the body and assists us with letting go of negative and unhelpful thinking. To really listen, our focus must be at a deeper level of what's being communicated, along with some degree of emotional sensitivity. Creating an atmosphere of openness, broad-mindedness, and an unconditional view of others supports deep listening and wise communication.

In some cultures, listening is considered a spiritual art form essential to nurturing shared responsibility and compassionate actions. Awareness of our own ambiguity and criticism allows us to acknowledge differences and let go of presumptions, an approach to listening that leads us into a place of curiosity, flexibility, and a genuine spirit of inquiry. One such listening practice is *dadirri*, the ancient aboriginal practice of connecting and inherent within their culture to maintain harmony. It teaches patience, silent waiting and how to be at peace as a way of life.

When we are able to listen more carefully and with focused attention, our idealized version of how things should be in accordance with what we have heard begins to dissipate, opening the way for letting go of our preconceived notions. Rather than just repeating habitual reactions or scripts from past experiences, the act of deep listening creates an internal map which can expand our capacity for communicating and understanding. If we sit with others and listen, with our hearts and minds, we find that the words we thought we ought to say, or planned on saying, may have changed. New words form; a different way of communicating our thoughts and ideas is blended with our insights. Deep listening is critical if we are to embrace the idea that each person's experience is uniquely important and valid.

Understanding and practicing deep listening and wise speech is key to finding common ground. We need to practice empathetic and compassionate forms of communication which do not create the illusion of separation. We can learn to communicate in ways where we can change our hearts and minds if need be, and give life to vibrant voices. Tending to both commonalities and differences calls us to communicate skillfully, creating a foundation for meaningful relationships. When we can listen with awareness and speak with everyone's best interests in mind, there is the possibility to transform our understanding of ourselves and others into acts of compassion and good will.

STORIES THAT MATTER

Jeannette Armstrong, PhD
Richard Reoch
Ibu Robin Lim, CPM

JEANNETTE ARMSTRONG, PHD

Jeannette Armstrong, PhD is a steward of the earth
and knowledge keeper of the Okanagan Syilx people,
whose traditional territory spans parts of Washington
State and British Columbia. She is a proponent of protecting
cultural traditions and bringing the values of protecting the
earth and honoring different views and opinions into her
actions. The importance of community, family, and the earth
are expressed through teaching stories, and these inform her
work as activist and teacher. Jeannette speaks about diversity
and reciprocity and shares her perspective on doing no
harm when working with indigenous cultures.

"Language that takes into consideration
that there are different views, opinions, and
levels of knowledge on the subject."

The Syilx Okanagan people speak about themselves as those
that dream together—the dream, or the unseen part of
existence of human beings. Another way of looking at this is
if you take a number of strands of hair or twine, place them in
your hands and rub them together, they bind and become one
strand. We use this thought symbolically when we make twine,
thread, and coiled baskets. This refers to our being tied into and
part of everything else, and to the dream parts of us that form
our community. The Syilx Okanagan refers to relationships
with others through a word that means "our one skin."

To do no harm is our social ethic. We can and will engage in the
defense of our community, family, and land. The Syilx Okana-

gan language has principles founded on the idea of respecting diversity. It uses language that takes into consideration different views, opinions, and levels of knowledge on any given subject. Using noncoercive language clarifies one's reasoning and choices. Our people express compassion as being inspired, to be in joy, and in a state of bliss.

We form our ethics and values using images of living things from the land. This imagery is represented in our teaching stories. The Syilx Okanagan oral language is not abstract. It provides symbolic meaning. The animistic images in these stories are the way meaning is constructed. The story characters carry knowledge and become real living family members, maybe more so. These are beloved characters that emanate guidance, compassion, joy, and love. So if we grow up with the language, we grow up experiencing a level of joy, love, and celebration as a part of nature and our being. If this language is taken away, it is like someone coming in to shoot your grandmother or grandfather, who have bestowed kindness and warmth upon you.

In every circumstance, people must be seen in their unique and specific context. Equality is thought of as the right of all persons to be understood, respected, and treated in an unbiased manner within the knowledge of their unique and specific context. This becomes our right, no matter who we are, to physical and psychological well being and fulfillment. Our most serious teaching is that community comes first, then family, and then ourselves as individuals, because without community and family, we are not truly human. To have a healthy community, the Okanagan believe there needs to be an emotional response between people's interactions—a communing. To be without community in this way is to be alone and only alive in the flesh. When this occurs, it becomes possible to violate and destroy others and their property without remorse.

Euro-Western society is blind to the way they create "other" or the idea of "other." They create hierarchy by the expected framework that comes from media, television, or conversation with others. One of the strangest ideas of Euro-Western society is the lack of acceptance of people that are "nobody" as opposed to people that are "somebody." This system puts people in one of these categories that can either disempower you or make you disappear altogether in terms of your identity. People do it without knowing they are doing it. In the Okanagan way of life there is a resistance to that kind of privileged hierarchical standing.

Some Okanagans want to change how our government and our decision process works, but that is creating conflict and harm in our community. For instance, in the Western construct, a chief is someone that makes decisions for the people. However, in the Okanagan community, that was never the traditional role of the Chief. In our culture one must make compromises and recognize the rights of others in a beautiful, respectful, and willing way. This happens from a deep level of understanding of the human situation. Traditionally, an Okanagan Chief brings the people together, listens to them, and finds a way to meet all of their concerns within a collaborative dialogue. This is a process of inclusion to make sure everyone is informed. The Chief sorts out priorities related to the needs of the people, and then shares these priorities with the community.

The biggest obstacle to our way of life is that people on the outside believe they have the answers without considering our communities' differences. For instance, in social work, the idea that illness is larger than the individual can be a difficult process for social workers dealing with some of our community issues. Okanagans believe that health issues are an expression of the family, not just the individual. It is rarely approached that way by outsiders. how First Nation family systems work within a closed community is something that is often met with resistance and sometimes violence.

In the language of Syilx Okanagans there is an equivalent word to compassion. It is action-based and literally means "to take in internally the knowledge of an injustice" and emotionally sense that someone or something is being harmed. Okanagans believe responsibility and understanding your relationship to others is the essence of compassion. It is essential to resolve injustices and provide support to those in need. My people would not walk away from a stranger lying on the street. They would help them as if they were a close loved one. Compassion is not just something we feel, it is something we act on because we must. In our culture, the more direct actions one takes to assist, support, and protect others without compromise—even to their own danger, loss, or threat—the more that person becomes whole and healthy.

RICHARD REOCH

Is it possible to work in ways that do no harm? Richard Reoch helps expand our understanding of this concept as he shares his observations and experiences as a spiritual practitioner, philosopher, leader, and international peace builder. While reality, context, and effort are fundamental to our work, he also speaks to the importance of using our language and listening in ways that do not create barriers. Richard reminds us that mindfulness is a way to access this deep knowing translated into right action.

"The actual teaching [of the Buddha] is to be utterly, totally, and completely inclusive."

It is not easy to do no harm. Even when you are making every effort to cause no harm, people may experience what you do as harmful, for reasons unknown to you, and possibly to them as well. Some traditions stress the importance of intention, on the basis that while you cannot be held responsible for all of the effects of your actions, you can do everything in your power to act from the intention to benefit others or do no harm. This is easier said than done, since both intention and action arise in a social, cultural, and political context where there are very different viewpoints about what is harmful or beneficial. In my experience, an attitude of "doing your best in the circumstances," and realizing that this is what virtually everyone else is doing (whether we agree with what they do or not), is somewhat more manageable. It relieves us of the multiple burdens or expectations of being absolutely right, being completely consistent, and making no mistakes. At the same time, it acts as a constant reminder to "raise our gaze" and be considerate in the midst of the flux and confusion of daily life.

I have seen a number of situations where people from outside organizations come to partner with local organizations. Often, they bring with them a considerable number of cultural assumptions that they believe are true and applicable in all situations. They seek, from the beginning, to impose these assumptions on the local situation with extraordinary insensitivity. As a result, I have seen real wreckage. I have also seen workers from outside organizations assume that they have a God-given mandate to deal with all the problems, rather than the one problem they were asked to come in to help repair. I think that people who want to take this kind of all-encompassing approach should be clear that this is their intention from the outset. Personally, I am in favor of a much more humble approach, rather than imposing a cultural worldview. That's not fair for anyone.

It's very important not to idealize this kind of work: this practice. When people talk about being present, or a feeling of being present, it can sound like a wonderful experience. I find it helpful to think in terms of uncertainty and discomfort. We tend to be trained to equate certainty with intelligence, so if we don't know what's going on, we feel we're lacking or inadequate. Many people in their search for self-worth search for certainty, particularly a certainty they can articulate. If you're working in a team or a highly intellectual environment, you may have to speak like that in order to have your colleagues think you have good judgment. But in fact, the person who can endure and keep their mind open in a situation where they don't know, or they can't say exactly what is happening, what to think or what to say, may well be the person who has the possibility of contributing the most.

Everybody has a tendency to want a physical or emotional comfort and that's not really being offered in this line of work. That tendency has the unfortunate quality of closing down the inquiry and curiosity and the ability to remain present. The most important time to be able to be present is when things are the most uncertain and the most uncomfortable, because at the extreme part of uncertainty and discomfort, lie the greatest moments for potential change.

I think rather than my own opinion on the matter, let's look at what the Buddha said about mindfulness. He said it is the path of understanding that the nature of the mind is already full, complete, and enlightened. Every single human being, no matter what his or her karma or suffering, has an enlightened mind.

We should be very careful in creating our own conceptual barriers to think that there are others who, because of their karma, are somehow inferior. The fundamental teaching of mindfulness is one of the greatest teachings on equality that is imaginable—that the nature of our mind is inherently fully awakened, immediately accessible, and contained in every single being. It's important because I meet people who think this whole idea of enlightenment applies to everybody except bankers, except people who engage in domestic violence, except terrorists, except people serving in the military. If they're homophobic, it's everyone except people who are gay or lesbian. There is always a group which is set aside. The actual teaching is to be utterly and totally completely inclusive.

"Every person is a stream whose origin is unknown," says a Hindu text. This is a wonderful basis for contemplating compassion. Seeing one's self and others as a stream of experience, much of which is unknown or mysterious, both to others and ourselves, gives rise to natural humbleness and open-mindedness. Without these qualities, it is possible for our attitudes and actions to be narrow-minded, prescriptive, and self-righteous, while imagining that they are compassionate.

The way things "really are" is experienced differently by people according to many factors, including their karmic inclinations, previous experiences, the context in which they are having the experience, and how they see things fitting into their world view. Thus, making an effort to understand the experience of other people could be said to be supremely important in living with them, working with them, and also being in conflict with them. The wisdom of seeing things as they really are arises from understanding that each person's experience is unique to them. Working in this way seems to open the door to compassionate, skillful action.

One of the most important aspects of engaging with other people and situations—perhaps the most fundamental aspect of all—is being willing and able to listen to them. To accomplish this requires mindfulness. You need to be aware of your own mental habits, such as subliminally judging what the other person is saying instead of giving them your undivided and full attention. You need to be able to be fully present to what the other person is communicating. That includes their words, but also everything else that is being expressed without words. These two forms of mindfulness can only be practiced if you are able to be with the other person in the present moment and return again to the present whenever your attention has strayed.

I feel that listening is a lost art. Perhaps it's never been there. Many of us now inhabit a world where the chaos and speed and information flow to which we are perpetually subject has become so intense that we've actually become de-skilled in listening. Often, I have had the opportunity to watch people fail at this kind of work—in small ways and in big ways. People continually ask me, "What is your brilliant advice based on all this experience?" If you were to ask me if I saw a common factor in what has led to the breakdown of relationships, or the inability to resolve a problem, I am embarrassed to say, I have an incredibly simple answer to this. In my experience, it has always been a failure of listening.

This goes back to the question of mindfulness because in order to be able to listen, you have to be aware of what's going on in your own head. Since what's going on is not listening but a range of other activities, you can't even get to first base in the world of listening because you have yet to realize the mind is engaged in other activities. And then to cultivate listening and go beyond just hearing, to a deeper level of appreciating what's being communicated, requires some level of emotional sensitivity. It requires what some call patience, but I'm more inclined to say it is a clear effort to set oneself aside.

Setting aside the expectation that you will experience or receive hope, joy, and love in your work seems to be a precondition for wise and considerate action. Otherwise, when you experience disappointment, there is a tendency to blame others and feel resentful. An approach of doing your best without being emotionally dependent on any particular outcome seems to create an atmosphere of great openness, broad-mindedness, and unconditional accommodation of others.

Once, I wanted to engage with a highly regarded senior religious figure that was known to be extremely sensitive to one side of a war. There had been very little progress in stopping this war. I decided to take ten days and go to the place where he lived. I took nothing with me and just hung out with him in the complete uncertainty and discomfort of that place, never raising any questions with him. After the eighth day, he turned to me and asked if I wanted to go for a ride in his car. We drove into the countryside in silence. After a while he said, "This war is the greatest burden in my heart." At that point, we had crossed the threshold.

What eventually causes people to cross over some threshold, a threshold that they might not be able to define, but that which is at least as high and forbidding as the gigantic wall that separates Israel and Palestine? It's not predictable, and it's, on some level, not analyzable. It functions at a very deep level of the psyche, which is closer to our emotional life than our logical life. To cross that threshold in the mind and heart towards, in some cases, even the possibility of reconciliation is a mysterious process.

IBU ROBIN LIM, CPM

Robin Lim is a proponent of gentle birth and has been referred to as a guerilla midwife for her work in delivering babies in environmental disaster zones and warzones. She shares her insights into human resiliency and the importance of hope and love in creating a more peaceful and compassionate world.

"I feel that pulling one's hope very close, and embracing it as a part of joy, can be done."

Words are powerful. They can be medicine or they can do great harm. I feel like I—as a mother, grandmother, midwife, team leader, partner—am always learning to use my words well. I suggest to everyone that they learn at least one language other than the one they normally speak. This helps slow one down verbally, and the poetry and healing qualities of your words can better emerge as one navigates the waters of a new language.

The beauty of being a BirthKeeper, a midwife, of sitting with mother and baby as they make the amazing journey through labor, birth, and postpartum, is that one must be present, mindful, and heartful. Being with mother and baby, moment by moment, in support of the gentle, natural unfolding of the miracle of birth, is a blessing indeed. If there is a situation that puts mother or baby at risk, the BirthKeeper must be super in the moment, highly mindful, to be able to make wise decisions in the event that lifesaving effective actions must be taken. I would say that as a BirthKeeper I have been blessed to participate at childbirth in the present, not the past, nor the future. Birth is right now. This focus happens when the StarGate opens to allow a baby's body and soul to come earthside. I call this the zone—that quiet, restful, alert state from which blessed decisions and actions arise.

Compassion is simply necessary if one is to be a BirthKeeper. Because I attend birth in disaster zones, any thought of my own suffering pales, disappears, and is forgotten. When I am with people who have barely any food or water, and inadequate shelter at best, I truly believe in the strength and resilience of humanity. These survivors of tsunami, earthquake, and super storms are not complaining. They are pulling together and helping one another to rise up and live well. It's easy to love and have compassion in the middle of a life such as mine.

At the StarGate between life and death, there is only equality. I tend to be a person who cannot bear injustices. When I must witness inequality, it's hard to endure. Much of my work is to lobby for human rights in childbirth. In the context of witnessing birth in highly medically driven settings, I observe that women have little power over what happens to them, and babies have none. Right at the time of childbirth, women are so open, so vulnerable; it seems a huge injustice that medical professionals would be less than compassionate at such a critical time.

As a midwife, I must see things as they are, for sometimes it is a matter of life or death. For example, diagnosing a super high-risk pregnancy that is best managed in the hospital. I would prefer for all mothers and babies to have gentle births in birth centers, like Bumi Sehat or at home. However, some births are best handled in the hospital. At the same time, it's important that I hold an optimistic point of view. I must believe in each expectant mother's potential to manifest her miracle, her way. This means I believe in standing on three feet—good science of medicine, respect for nature, and holding a space for spirit or faith—whatever makes the mother feel safe. If we rely only on science, too many mothers will endure highly technical births like cesareans. I feel that from the point of view of standing firmly on three strong feet, I can best see things as they really are.

Joy for pregnant women is so important because cortisol, the hormone of sadness and stress, inhibits brain growth for the gestating baby in the womb. So a pregnant woman who experiences plenty of joy will have a more intelligent baby. Hope is a bit tricky. It's like a carrot on a stick. I feel that pulling one's hope very close and embracing it as a part of joy can be done. I try to do this in my day-to-day life, especially if I am concerned about something in the near future. For example, a mother has climbing blood pressure and she's soon to have her baby. Nothing we advise her to do, and no medications or treatments or herbs or homeopathy seem to help. I have to hope all will be well.

Even stronger than that hope is setting my intention and prayers on the future. I envision this mother and this baby in perfect happiness and bliss and safety after the birth. I breathe this vision in and out as if my hope has already come true, like a wish fulfilled. I also take good steps to accomplish this wish with the mother. I have in recent years made it a habit to have morning meetings of only a few moments or minutes. In the meetings I acknowledge my angels, thank them for the help that is so obvious to me, and ask them for more help—outlining their tasks, assigning them to look after people, and more. It seems to be working!

Working in ways that do no harm is a huge question for a midwife and a BirthKeeper because every second of every minute, every hour on earth, doctors, midwives, and nurses are harming newborn babies. As an example, there are issues around the practice of immediately clamping and cutting babies' umbilical cords. This is a huge human rights issue and crosses all borders. When a woman enters nearly any hospital or health care facility to have her baby, at the moment of birth her child's umbilical cord will be clamped and cut. Research has clearly given no justification for this intervention, which is considered to be too abrupt. Research has proven that the delay of umbilical cord severance is beneficial. Up to one-third of a baby's blood is still transitioning from the placenta to the baby via the umbilical cord at the time of birth. Children may not donate blood. Adults may only give 10% at any given time and under strict guidelines. Yet hospitals are robbing newborn babies of up to 33% of their blood supply. The blood in the umbilical cord at the time of birth is not cord blood, but baby's blood. Many hospitals sell this cord blood, which is in fact baby blood needed by each baby for optimal health and intelligence. Doctors, midwives, and nurses must stop harming babies. We do take an oath to never do harm, and it's time we really look at any medically sanctioned bad habits and practices that are not evidence-based and strive to practice obstetrical medicine with kindness.

In my work as a midwife, I witness the miracles of love day and night. Love is essential. It is kind and strong while being gentle. Love manifests as the hormone oxytocin and was present when we were conceived. It is considered the hormone of love and must be abundant for birth to be accomplished. Love really does make the world go round. It's so rewarding and, in fact, fun to be an advocate for love, which is what every mother, grandmother, and BirthKeeper is.

THE PRACTICE OF WISE SPEECH AND DEEP LISTENING

CONSIDER THIS

▶ Listen to what is being said and ask questions with a genuine spirit of inquiry. Put your phone away at dinner, become part of the conversation, and ask how the day went.

▶ Taking time to be silent and quietly listening helps us hear what is being said in a more open way.

▶ Letting go of ambiguities, criticisms, and judgments can allow you to truly listen and speak wisely.

▶ And remember to listen more and talk less.

NOW ASK YOURSELF

▶ How can I pay attention while listening to others?

- What does it take for me to really listen to someone?

- What causes me to be unfocused in conversations or while listening to others speak?

- Am I distracted by thinking about other things when in a conversation?

- How can I stay curious and engaged in conversations that are all too familiar?

- How can I reserve judgement in conversations that are completely unfamiliar? Is it possible for me to put aside my assumptions, criticisms, opinions and judgments and listen and speak without bias?

▶ Is it possible for me to demonstrate an openness and willingness to pay attention to the words I use?

- In difficult conversations, how can I use my words to reflect what I have heard without harming others?

- How might I use words that convey I am open to changing my mind?

- How can I respond when what is being communicated differs from my own values and beliefs?

- Do you have people in your life you would like to be able to communicate with in a different way? If so, what might that look like?

▶ Are there mindful engagement qualities that I can bring into the way I communicate?

- How would a conversation be different if I was to be more authentic?

- If I were more mindful, could I do a better job of paying attention on purpose?

- Could I use my words and listen in such a way that demonstrates more compassion and kindness?

- Might I find ways to bring more happiness and joy into my communication with friends, colleagues and family?

NOW PRACTICE

▶ Listening to Create Possibilities Rather than Limitations

- Ask a trusted person to give you feedback on the way you communicate with them.

- When in a conversation with someone, practice being attentive. Notice if there is anything keeping you from listening deeply and responding with clarity and non-judgment. Jot down what those barriers might be.

- Pay attention to conversations where you are trying to listen to what someone else is saying, yet you are predicting how the conversation will play out. Notice whether or not this interferes with your understanding of what they were trying to communicate.

- In the future, how might you practice communicating without bias?

- Journal about a person you were recently in a difficult conversation with. What made you feel uneasy about what you heard? How did you respond to what was being said?

▶ Communicating to Find Common Ground

- It's difficult to find common ground with someone when we have failed to skillfully communicate with them. Identify a person you want to reconcile a difference with or a situation where consensus is needed. Begin by working together to find words or phrases that represent how you'd like to engage with each other now and in the future. For example: respectful, kind, clear, collaborative, honest. Write down those words. Now agree to listen to your respective stories and points of view related to the matter at hand. You can only ask questions of each other and refrain from interrupting or providing a rebuttal.

- Once you've spent time using your words wisely and listening deeply, discuss the shared experiences that emerged from this conversation. Do this by reflecting back words you used and what you heard each other say.

- Has this changed your understanding of how this disagreement came to be and how resolution or consensus might be reached?

▶ Creating a Community of Practice

- Set some time aside with friends, family, or colleagues for a discussion that focuses on a subject of mutual interest related to social or political issues. (We suggest you start with social issues and move, gently, into political ones!)

- Bring your attention to the quality of wise speech and deep listening before you begin.

- Ask the group how they think skillful communication can contribute to living and working in ways that do not harm.

THE QUALITY OF MINDFULNESS
PAYING ATTENTION ON PURPOSE

You do not need to know precisely what is
happening, or exactly where it is all going. What
you need is to recognize the possibilities and
challenges offered by the present moment and to
embrace them with courage, faith, and hope.

—FATHER THOMAS MERTON

*M*indfulness is the balanced awareness and acceptance
of the present experience without creating stories or
judgements that may cause misunderstandings or actions
which we might regret.

While, historically, mindfulness has roots in Buddhism, other
traditions use similar systems such as contemplative prayer,
rituals, and ceremonies. These are ways of paying attention
to one's inner and outer world. A system that has been used
for over 2,500 years in many traditions, mindfulness is com-
monly referred to as a practice of meditation that enhances
our skills to monitor and consciously balance the mind and
body systems. Most important to remember is that mindfulness can be practiced by anyone and is not dependent on
ideological views or spiritual and religious beliefs.

The practical application of mindfulness has become a way to
relieve physical and emotional pain, manage stress, improve

self-regulation, and foster compassion and empathy. It is being used by professionals in many fields. Conflict resolution practitioners, healthcare providers, social workers, governmental and non-governmental organizations, and the military have recognized the value of mindfulness practice. Verified by numerous scientific studies, mindfulness meditation develops the social circuits of the brain that cultivate compassion for self and others. This suggests that mindful states may play an important role, not only in coping with difficult experiences, but in building the brain's capacity for universal compassion and kindness.

Being aware of one's thoughts and emotions is the first step in recognizing how easily we get distracted and lose connection to what is happening right in front of us. And while the present moment may be filled with pleasant experiences, it may also be filled with dread, helplessness and uncertainty. Seeing violence in the streets, threats of autocracy, the demise of democracy or families without access to basic human needs are not exceptions. We are witnessing atrocities on a daily basis. Our 'present moment' is often filled with enormous challenges. Being mindful in both situations helps us become more thoughtful and view our emotions and reactions through deliberate and heightened observation.

As we develop wisdom and qualities of engagement that can be applied in our lives and our work, it is important to refine our awareness. Mindfulness can help inform our actions and allow us to reach a clearer understanding of how thoughts and emotions can impact the ways we respond to the conditions that surround us. The contemplative practice of mindfulness invites us to bring our attention to the constant stream of events which in turn, allows us to move through life in a gentler, kinder, and more effective way. Mindfulness can be helpful in revealing our attachment to certain beliefs and stories—attachments that can affect the choices we make and the actions we take. It can also enrich our experiences and give us skills to respond in troubling times. Being more mindful also supports the groundwork for mutual respect and good communication. Through the practice of mindfulness, we can learn to identify what makes us uncomfortable or fearful and recognize what limits our capacity to act from our best intentions.

Mindfulness is intricately linked to our ability to be compassionate and the feelings that arise from our suffering and the suffering of others. As we witness suffering, there is a need for us to be fully present and allow for a natural transparency and openness to recognize our own suffering. This is especially critical when we experience emotional reactivity. When faced with unexpected and potentially explosive encounters, our fight or flight behavior is activated. We tend to either withdraw or become increasingly tense and shift into high gear. And when this happens, it is possible for our thinking, perceiving and acting, to be compromised.

Practicing mindfulness can cultivate an inner balance and clarity as a way to support our efforts and good deeds. Seen as a core process in informing the human experience of introspection and self-inquiry, mindfulness is fundamental to giving us a wider lens from which to view our various experiences. When we are able to integrate mindfulness into our personal and professional lives, we can pay attention to who we are and who others may be in a uniquely different way. We create a delicate balance as we become clear, aware, calm and self-assured. This allows us to recognize the subtleties and complexities of our interactions that are often required in critical situations and challenging environments. The ability to see things as they unfold for what they are and in a direct and immediate way can be helpful. We need to see that which is true for ourselves and for others in order to respond in a way that addresses the issue at hand with clarity and responsibility. Deepening our awareness of the moment becomes a source and guide for how we engage, and ultimately how we take actions that are meaningful and effective. Mindfulness practice asks us to not merely be 'present in the moment', but to train our minds so we can deepen our inquiry into our thought patterns and belief systems and how they affect our actions.

There is a story about a student who comes to his spiritual teacher and announces his desire to become enlightened. The teacher says to the student, "Go to your backyard and dig a well." The student responds, "Is that all I have to do?" And the teacher replies, "Yes." So the student goes to his backyard and begins to dig a hole but cannot find water. He goes to another spot and begins to dig, but still there is no water. Then he digs another hole and another until the entire backyard looks like it has craters in it, but there is still no water. The student goes back to the teacher and says, "I dug for water, but there wasn't any water to be found." The teacher asks, "Did you go deep in any of them?"

In situations that are filled with uncertainty and chaos, the practice of mindfulness can be very helpful, reminding us to acknowledge, pause, breathe, and check our energy and our intentions. As mindful awareness develops, our actions can transform the often-confused energy of emotions, both ours and others, into clarity of the situation at hand. As we engage in ways that are mindful, we experience a new opening within ourselves, a spaciousness that allows us to bring our whole heart and mind, along with our full attention to the situation at hand.

STORIES THAT MATTER

Shantum Seth
Phyllis Schafer Rodriguez
Mayumi Oda

SHANTUM SETH

Whether leading pilgrimages through the heart of India to witness the path of the Buddha or spearheading international efforts to incorporate mindfulness as a way of supporting teachers, Shantum work as an advocate for human rights and peacemaking has been a lifelong practice. As a Buddhist teacher in the lineage of Thich Nhat Hanh, he has inspired many on their path to touch the suffering of all people and practice peace.

"This interconnectedness is so embedded in the reality of existence that social and universal responsibility becomes enlightened self-interest."

After working as a social activist for many years, and getting burned out in the process, I wanted to find a way to *be peace* rather than create peace. I needed more reflection, so I went to all sorts of teachers—Native American, Hindu, Muslim, Christian. Finding Buddhism to fit my temperament, I met Thich Nhat Hanh in 1986. He taught me to touch peace, opening the door to mindfulness for me as energy you cultivate in everything you do. It really helps us respond rather than react. Another important element in this practice was the importance of a group to work with—a *sangha*—which is very important in order to not become isolated in our work and go for the long term.

Much of what is important as we engage in ways that do no harm develops over time as you practice mindfulness. Compassion, all of these qualities, grow as you become more mindful. You can take any of these qualities of mindful engagement and place them in the spokes of a wheel and, if you practice, they all link. They don't grow independently. In the center of the spoke, you need stillness. The outside of the wheel is filled with action. We are engaged with some of the worst realities you can come across—discrimination, murder, poverty, and serious illness. This is the outer wheel. Inside, if I don't find that stillness, I can start creating a mess. My issues get into the outer circle. I didn't realize that until I started becoming part of the problem through my anger, my activism. When I was 23 years old, I was elected Vice President of the student union in England. I was very involved in social action. I'd gone to jail opposing the stationing of U.S. cruise missiles in England and anti-apartheid issues. There was a lot of active anger associated with my activist nature. My efforts were all focused outward, yet there was no nurturing of myself. I needed this nurturing of myself as well as a greater spiritual connection.

I started going to different teachers and then happened to end up in a retreat in the western U.S. with Thich Nhat Hanh. He led us in a practice of walking meditation and, for the first time, I experienced peace. My non-separateness and harmony with nature, what is all around me and what is inside of me gave me the impetus to carry on. I moved back to India with this practice as a base to help with understanding who I am, my own authenticity, my stillness, my limits, my ability to look at my own feelings. Since then, I have used mindfulness as a practice. When I got back into social action, I had a much greater sense of self. What I try to do all the time is not harming. If you look at the mindfulness training of Thich Nhat Hanh, everything we do is like that. Working from the precept of "don't harm" and try not to make things worse.

A few years ago, there was a big terrorist action in Mumbai.

A hotel was bombed and many people were killed. We were watching television in Delhi, and I got very angry. Because of my practice, I was able to stop, take a walk in the garden, and look at the flowers, realizing they were still beautiful. I started reflecting on one of the terrorists—who he may be, why he did this. What came out of this reflection was a young man raised in an impoverished home, fed a lot of ideologically based propaganda and monetary inducements for his family. My mind moved from an anger state to a compassionate state—not that I was going to act, but the potential for action is very great at this point, especially as I saw the knee-jerk reaction of others around the world. We have to look at the roots of these sorts of things with compassion, not this man and his last act. When you are in a situation of suffering, witnessing, or part of something, normally what happens is you come into a more silent space initially—a space where you can be more present as to what is happening, rather than letting your own ideas and perceptions take over. When this may be happening in any situation—the death of someone close to you, an accident, you meet someone dying on the road—it's really important to stay present and centered. In India there are a lot of things going on where one can help. Sometimes it becomes overwhelming. We need a sense of calm in the midst of turmoil. It is like the story of the boat people from Vietnam where everyone starts panicking and one person stays calm and subsequently keeps the boat from capsizing.

In situations of difficulty I feel it is quite important to stay humble. Humility is a very important quality for social action. Whenever I go to work in a village, for example, I always feel like I am getting far more than I am giving, and I try to instill this in volunteers. In this kind of work, don't think you're going to be a do-gooder. The person who is gaining the most is you, by developing your mindfulness, your compassion. Ultimately, you're helping yourself. You act in the context, not just from a blanket solution, but you must be skillful at that time and in the moment. For example, drinking water is a good action, but if you drink water after a stomach operation you might die.

I think that we act a lot from our intuition. We might think that we act from our brain or calculated ideas, but when you come into most situations, you act from somewhere deep in your gut. Over time, you start trusting this more and more. It comes when you're more silent. It's a bit like when you're meditating and your mind is calm, a thought arises and you see things for what they are. This intuitive wisdom arises. As you cultivate your mind, intuition becomes more present. The real insights and creative wisdom comes forward in order to act in ways that do no harm.

Living in India is so multifaceted. In some ways it's organized chaos. When I travel on these pilgrimages, I go into situations, for example, with twenty-four-hour traffic jams and huge crowds that you can't imagine. I have to engage people in human ways—nonaggressive, helping people understand why they are doing what they are doing. I must always remember that I am engaging with another human being, especially in India where they are so stratified in castes—woman or man, Hindu or Muslim, and things of that sort. I look at everyone without a discriminating eye and always try to empathize with the suffering of others so I can understand this through always being present with an open heart and calm mind.

Mindfulness is this presence of mind, this attentiveness, and this compassion that are what I understand to be mindfulness in its purest form. In India, things are always shifting. It is a very complex society—politically, socially, and religiously. Living here is a dance. I see that mindfulness helps me to stay centered and come back to my breathing. Whenever something is happening that is beyond my comprehension, I go back to my breathing to create and build the space that allows me to respond, rather than react. Unfortunately, mindfulness is being used more now as a technique, but it is like an energy that you're cultivating through a presence more than anything else. It's a slow drip system of mind cultivation happening over many years.

I'm reminded of a very nice story. I was on a pilgrimage with Thich Nhat Hanh. We were in a favorite place of the Buddha in India with all these beggar children hanging around. They are very good at begging. Yet, instead of giving something to this one child, Thich Nhat Hanh held one of her hands and told me to hold the other. It was one of these beautiful urchin kids. her hand was cupped from holding it out that way for so long to beg, but after a few minutes, her hand released into softness as she held our hands. A simple act.

What I have found is that looking at these people has shifted my perception of begging. It helps shift our lens on poverty, beauty, and all of those things. We see beggars, leprosy, people without arms, and I always say to the pilgrims in our journey, "They are here as your teachers." When you see these things, it is important to see what comes up for you. Is it compassion? Is it disgust? Is it anger, guilt, or love? Rather than giving, pay attention, because giving in many ways kills that feeling. After a short time, the pilgrims come forward with really wise solutions and ways to be of value, rather than simply giving the beggars money or food right away. Giving itself can be done unwisely.

One of the *paramitas*—actions for liberation—is *dana*, or dona-tion, but again, not done without wisdom. What the Buddha suggests is that you give so that you touch the suffering of others and you become that—her suffering is your suffering, and his poverty is your poverty. You do it in such a way that you touch it, not give it. This is connected to the concept of interconnected-ness or interbeing. This informs a lot of my work. My suffering is your suffering, and your suffering is my suffering. We are not separate. The level of commonality is much greater than the level of difference. The other thing I find helpful is the Four Noble Truths and the question, "What is the cause of suffering?"

Deep listening is a very important part of right speech, espe-cially when there are people trying to share their suffering. If you simply listen to them, half the problem is solved. Listening helps heal them. The other part is not telling lies, exaggerating, or telling someone one thing and another person something else. Also it is important for us to not use harsh language, but try to be humble in our speech—trying to not be a "know-it-all." People come to you looking for answers, and in a way, it's eas-ier to tell them what to do. But it's more important to facilitate rather than be directive. Tone is very important; letting peo-ple feel that you are empathetic. Authenticity is important, as well as a way of bringing honesty to our speech. Words are like medicine sometimes—the taste may be bitter, but the result is helpful. Things must be said with an open heart. You have to keep a sort of mind where you don't lose a part of your heart and allow for others to not lose their hearts.

Equanimity, for me, is key to mindful engagement. India is a great test. You have to live and practice this quality of stay-ing balanced while not getting caught in the highs and lows of emotions, otherwise you go mad. The nature of reality is that with the highs also comes the lows. Also, equanimity is an essential element in our ability to work, as well as our spiritual practice. We shouldn't make it such that we become unfeeling, because there is a risk that if you don't touch the feelings, you become immune. We can avoid this by realizing that each feeling arises and falls away, so the practice is to experience it the way it is. You don't devalue the feeling. You experience it, but don't react to the feeling.

As you get more and more tuned into this interbeing nature of reality, you realize that other people's happiness is your happiness. If my wife is not happy, I am not happy. If my neighbor is not happy, his problems spill over into my house. If my neighboring country is not happy, we are unhappy. This interconnectedness is so embedded in the reality of existence that social and universal responsibility becomes enlightened self-interest. It comes from a sense that there is no separation. It happens with practice and becomes second nature. Yet living in a country like India, you have to be careful that you don't lose your compassion, because there is so much need, so much difficulty and you can lose your ability to act. It's an interesting dance not to get caught in the "me, mine, I." This is part of the flow and the "I" is the static part. The basis of our suffering is the over-identification of the "I." "I need to do this. I need to fix this," is the cause of much suffering. In India, the word for doing no harm is *ahimsa*—non-harming. For our own, enlightened self-interest, we have to have responsibility for not harming.

PHYLLIS SCHAFER RODRIGUEZ

Responding to the loss of her son in the 9/11 World Trade Center tragedy, Phyllis Rodriguez speaks to nonviolence and forgiveness. Reaching across the aisle to others, even in the face of grief and adversity, gave Phyllis insight into how we can face difficult situations and, at the same time, work for peace and reconciliation through the practice of doing no harm.

"I've learned that one way to heal is to bridge the gap between between others and ourselves."

I don't define what I do as work. It is a part of my life and the way I try to make sense of the death of my son. When 9/11 happened, deep down we knew our government was going to do something that could end up being the biggest mistake in the world. This event became more than just a personal tragedy. We wondered if there was anything we could do at all regarding the outcry for military retaliation as a product of our overwhelming culture of revenge. My husband tried to send an open letter to *the New York Times* titled "Not In Our Son's Name," but it never made it there before circulating on the Internet. We emailed the letter to our friends to notify them about what had happened. Our friends emailed the letter to their friends, and their friends sent it to others. Very quickly, it went viral. We received letters in the mail from people living around the world and became aware that our voice was more powerful than it would have been if we had not lost our son.

My husband and I wrote that, when we first heard the news, we shared moments of grief, comfort, hope, despair, and fond memories with our daughter and daughter-in-law, family, friends, and neighbors. We could see our hurt and anger reflected in everybody we met. We couldn't pay attention to the daily flow of news about this disaster, but we read enough to sense that our government was heading in the direction of violent revenge and the prospect that people in distant lands would be dying, suffering, and nursing further grievances against our country. We feared that any such attacks would be justified in the name of our son and the almost three thousand others who perished that day. Our son's name would be used against the best interests of all of us. Our son died a victim of an inhuman ideology. Our nation should be thinking of rational responses to violent extremism that brings real peace and justice to our world instead of adding to the inhumanity of our times.

As a result of our letter, and several other letters circulating on the Internet by victims' family members calling for nonviolent solutions, we were put in touch with others of like mind. From these connections, September 11 Families for Peaceful Tomorrows was born on February 14, 2002. I have always been attracted to stories of people who reach across the aisle. In meeting with families that have lost children to violence, I have learned about compassion and empathy—when to respond, when to not say anything, and when to show support.

The most dramatic example of this is the day I met Aicha el-Wafi, a day that changed my life, because it changed my direction emotionally. It was the beginning of my learning that someone like Aicha, who has suffered so much, could still be emotionally generous. It brought out the generosity in me, and I felt better for it. Since then, I've learned that one way to heal is to bridge the gap between the "other" and ourselves.

In October 2001, Aicha's son, Zacarias Moussaoui, was indicted on six charges of conspiracy to commit violent acts related to the 9/11 attacks and faced the possibility of execution if convicted. Again, my husband and I wrote a letter to *the New York Times*, this time in opposition to the death penalty.

In November 2002, my husband and I and several other relatives of victims were invited by human rights workers to meet Aicha el-Wafi. When I met Aicha with others in a private room, no one knew what to say. I opened my arms and Aicha opened hers and we cried together—even though we had never met before. It seemed the most elemental way of making contact. Eventually, we went into a room and one person at a time shared their story. Through telling our stories we all were able to see each other as people who were suffering and who were joined by our mutual humanity and desire for peace. A Moroccan Muslim woman living in France and a secular Jewish woman living in the U.S. are no different when it comes to suffering. It was an accident of history that brought us together, and it is an accident of history that means Zacarias is now in prison and my son died in the World Trade Center. It could have been the reverse. When Greg was killed, I thought I would never forgive the people who murdered my son, but I have come to see forgiveness as more than a word. It's a context, a process. I don't forgive the act but trying to understand why someone has acted in the way they have is part of the process of forgiving. Forgiveness is being able to accept another person for being human and fallible, as we all are.

Since 2005, when Zacarias pleaded guilty to the conspiracy charges against him, I knew Aicha would be coming to America. I decided I wanted to give her as much support as I could beforehand. So we started speaking on the phone. I couldn't speak a word of French at that time, but somehow, we managed. Later, I continued supporting her in her campaign for the rights of her son, in the hope that someday he would be transferred to France to serve out his sentence.

Zacarias was an admitted member of al-Qaeda, but there's no evidence that he knew anything about the attacks on the World Trade Center. He pleaded guilty either because he felt it would get him more humane conditions of confinement, or because he was in no fit state to make any rational decisions. When I watched Zacarias at the trial, my heart was broken because I could not look at him as a stranger. I saw him as the son of my friend, Aicha. Meeting Aicha gave me strength and took away my anger and bitterness. It has also helped me to forgive myself, because a mother always feels guilty when things don't go right for her children.

My commitment to nonviolence and reconciliation has deepened since 2001. I am involved with the Westchester Martin Luther King, Jr. Institute for Nonviolence, as well as community and interfaith groups working for mutual understanding. Much of this was started in response to a disturbing rise of Islamophobia in New York and the nation. I also am part of a group helping formerly incarcerated men and women re-enter society. In 2006, I was introduced to healing of memories workshops led by Father Michael Lapsley of Cape Town, South Africa. He is a survivor of violence who received a letter bomb in retaliation for his anti-apartheid outspokenness. Through my continued connection with Father Michael and his work, I have had the opportunity to participate in workshops at Sing Sing Correctional Facility.

It is an inspiring experience for me when I hear stories from people serving time for serious crimes who are using their incarceration to grow as human beings and come to terms with their past lives. We listen to each other's stories and are moved to feel a connection to each other's suffering. They can empathize with me and I can express my admiration for their doing the difficult work of facing the consequences of their mistakes. Listening to them gives me insight into why some people do terrible things to others. We human beings all have the potential to change and learn from experience. This, and recognition of the universality of suffering, continually restores my hope for the future.

Recognizing that we all need each other is a big part of doing no harm. We all need acknowledgement and acceptance. Our goals should be to avoid knee-jerk reactions to situations (barring urgent or dangerous ones) and consider what would do no harm or as little as possible, such as diffusing anger or hostility when possible. It is also important that we not become so blinded by emotion or anger that we make things worse by failing to put ourselves in another's shoes, if even for the moment. I have not achieved a perfect record but continue my attempt to improve.

MAYUMI ODA

Mayumi Oda creates art as a pathway to change.
She has been involved in the antinuclear movement for more
than two decades and is devoted to living sustainably and
in a way that does not harm living things or the earth. She
shares her wisdom of mindfulness and engagement and their
contributions to individual and global transformation.

> "If you can really engage in everything
> you do, you see that your actions are
> part of the bigger universe."

I will speak about my work simply, because words for me are not enough to really get across my experience and how I work in the world. I convey the importance of life through my art. My art heals people because each painting is about our connection to each other, to the planet, and to something bigger than us. People are longing for that kind of connection. I do not want to name myself as a healer because people are their own best healers. However, when I make a painting, I am creating a doorway into healing. And when I speak about nuclear disarmament, it is the same thing—I am creating a doorway into healing by inviting people to wake up to what is in front of them, even if it is painful.

When you wake up to reality and what is before you in the moment, it is always kind. Even at death. You can get trapped in an idea of what is going to happen, but then your mind belongs somewhere else and not to the present. That is when you suffer. When you understand that reality is not a pre-scription and it is changing all the time, not fixed in some ideal, then you can relax into it and find your way through challenging situations.

Many Western people believe their thinking is something special, but it isn't. In my work I go into a room of people empty-handed to see what happens. I am patient, and I let whatever arises come forward. I have not always had that patience or presence. In fact, I was grieving my lack of patience for years. Now I recognize that mindfulness is everything within everyday life and in my work. If you can really engage in everything you do, you see that your actions are part of the bigger universe. Through this practice you become very sensitive to other people, all things, and to what is happening around you. This kind of mindfulness and engagement is the basis of right living. I use it all the time in cooking, eating, speaking, and painting. It is the connection to everything that creates mindfulness and brings us to the truth of what is right before us. Without this way of engaging, we can feel great loneliness and fear.

Doing no harm comes from the value of hope. If you lose it, you lose everything. It is the natural law of life. The act of seeing things in a positive way can pull you through and move you forward in the work you do, no matter how difficult it is. In fact, living and working from this place can transform the world.

Whatever action I do always includes thinking about the other from a place where I become empty and so big at the same time that I become the whole world. If you know you are part of the whole world, there is no separation, and your actions will come from your whole being. It is not like a prescribed medicine of how to do something—a recipe that tells you the step-by-step way to be. It is living and working moment by moment. This is the true heart of compassion in action.

THE PRACTICE OF MINDFULNESS

CONSIDER THIS

▶ Avoid distractions which tend to limit your capacity for introspection. Turn off the beeps of your phone. Try to find opportunities for being alone, quiet, and in nature.

▶ Nurture the parts of yourself that are kind and compassionate and look for ways to bring calmness, curiosity and creativity into your daily life.

▶ Release yourself from unhelpful patterns and choose to be present in the best way possible. When you think you have to *stay busy*, take a moment and when that thought occurs, pause, breathe and remind yourself that doing nothing can give you time to relax and let your mind rest.

▶ And remember, nothing is separate. We are all connected.

NOW ASK YOURSELF

▶ What thought patterns keep me from paying attention on purpose?

- Do I get distracted easily and stop paying attention? Or do I find my mind wandering and thinking about things outside of my current interaction and experience?

- Are there particular circumstances where I tend to lose focus? If so, might there be a pattern—on a video call, watching the news, with friends or colleagues who may have a different opinion (or the same opinion) about a certain issue? Something else?

- What might happen if I approached a difficult situation with awareness and flexibility rather than distraction or rigidity?

- How might my judgment, disappointment or fear get in the way of my ability to stay present? If someone has a different way of looking at something than my own, do I tend to want to interject my own attitudes, beliefs, or opinions before they are finished speaking?

▶ What contemplative practices can I incorporate into my daily life to help me live in the present moment?

- Which one or more of these could become a daily practice for me: meditation, prayer, yoga, singing, walking, gardening, cooking? Something else?

- When am I most calm? Is it when I'm gardening? Baking? Reading a book? Concentrating on a specific task at work? Playing with my kids?

- Can I find a place to spend time being quiet and contemplative, if even for a short time each day?

▶ How do my emotions affect my ability to pay attention on purpose?

- Do emotions, pleasant or unpleasant, contribute to how I respond? If so, how?

- When I have unpleasant feelings, is it hard for me to focus on what is important?

- What does feeling frustrated, disappointed or angry feel like in my body?

- How do I stay present in such a way that my negative emotions are turned into feelings that are constructive and useful?

▶ How might I develop open receptiveness?

- Knowing that if there's anything that's certain in life, it's that things will happen that are outside of my ability to control, can I stay open, willing, and pay attention to other points of view?

- What happens if I don't try to fix anything or need to control people or situations?

- When faced with unexpected encounters, do I withdraw, become increasingly tense, or do I become hyper vigilant and find it difficult to see things from other peoples' perspectives?

- If I were to imagine a difficult conversation where I allowed myself to be open-minded and willing to change my mind without regret, what might that look like?

NOW PRACTICE

▶ Focusing Your Attention

- There are a variety of mindfulness practices—meditating or walking, for example. You may already have a practice that works for you, or you may be a beginner. Whatever experience you have, be patient and know that it takes time and focus for you to be able to bring it into your life with ease.

- Check-in with yourself and identify what your mind is focused on. Is it wandering or focusing on the past, or planning for the future? Are you thinking about a disturbing story you read in yesterday's news? Are you planning what you will have for dinner or perhaps thinking about an important deadline? Whatever it might be, take a breath and choose to pay attention to what is happening right now. If you stick with it, does this change your experience?

- Journal about what distracts you from having focused attention. Explore the ways you get stuck in thought patterns and how it changes from moment to moment.

- Here is a practice to do at least once a day, starting with a minute or two: Bring your attention to your breathing. Notice the inhale, take a 3 second pause, notice the exhale. Continue to focus on your breath and take note of sounds, physical sensations, thoughts and emotions as they arise. Check in to see if your shoulders are tight, jaw clenched, hands gripping. Identify other places in your body where you are holding tension. Build up from once a day to three or four times each day.

- Here's another mindfulness practice: Bring your attention to the expansion of your chest with each inhale. Pay attention to how your chest contracts when you breathe out. Do this every day beginning with a period of 30 seconds and build up to longer periods to cultivate mindfulness.

▶ Using Mindfulness to Face Challenges and Stress

- Bring to mind a current challenge in your life that is causing you stress or emotional discomfort. Notice your body sensations, thought patterns and emotional reactions when you think of this situation. Does paying attention on purpose to your mind and body change the way you view this experience? If so, how?

- Tune into whatever negative feelings may be showing up and how those feelings and sensations make your body feel. If you feel tension in any part of your body, bring your focus to that area and do this relaxation exercise: take a breath, hold it for 3 counts, and exhale for 3 counts. Press your feet into the ground for 5 counts and breathe. This practice will help you focus and be present for the experience, moment by moment.

- Now, imagine that you are a still pond without any disturbance—no ripples or waves. What would that state of being look like with something that is causing you stress? Do you feel more peaceful? Are you able to stay balanced and relaxed? Or are you feeling restless?

▶ Creating a Community of Practice

- Set some time aside with friends, family, or colleagues for a discussion that focuses on a subject of mutual interest related to social or political issues. (We suggest you start with social issues and move, gently, into political ones!)

- Bring your attention to the quality of mindfulness before you begin.

- Ask the group how they think mindfulness can contribute to living and working in ways that do not harm.

THE QUALITY OF COMPASSION
A PATH TO ALTRUISM

Equal compassion is truly great compassion.

—CHAGDUD TULKU

Compassion is an outward expression exhibited towards our own suffering and the suffering of others. It is not cultivated simply for one's own sake, but more as an attitude of altruism toward all humanity. When we are able to understand, through compassion, our reasons for doing what we do, we are able to build this incredible bond of trust and safety. Compassion, in turn, allows us to cultivate equal regard for all people and their ways—*equanimity*—while maintaining a degree of composure and ability to remain calm and undisturbed, yet present and engaged.

There is a selfless, virtuous quality when we consider others' desire to be happy first and foremost, without jeopardizing our own happiness. The question of caring for others has been considered and debated from ancient days, as modern thinkers have advanced an ethic of virtue, care, and altruism. What if, at the forefront of our thoughts and actions, we could engage in deliberate ways that have the best interest of others in mind? Incorporating compassion and equanimity into our daily actions motivates us to act for all humanity, not solely for ourselves or those close to us.

By the very nature of being human, we are hardwired to connect, looking after the welfare of others and the planet with courage and conviction, compassion, and kindness. Yet, as we bring our knowledge and good intentions into the world, we can find ourselves overwhelmed with what we are witnessing and experiencing. Traumatic experiences, over-attending to the needs of others, and the inability to stay physically and emotionally safe can become hazards in our occupation and in our lives. We may experience alienation and fear. Our inclination is to step out of the intensity of suffering. However, when we realize what is at the heart of our suffering, and that of others, we are given a gift—the gift of compassion. It is this deep form of connection that liberates and moves us toward altruism.

Being compassionate is an active desire to alleviate suffering. Thomas Merton, a Catholic Trappist monk, modern religious writer, scholar, and philosopher, wrote extensively about both contemplative and social issues. He spoke to the inherent requirements for living a compassionate and merciful life. "Compassion," says Merton, "is not learned without suffering, nor is it easily attained nor understood." It is not something we simply do for ourselves. "The whole idea of compassion is based on a keen awareness of the interdependence of all these living beings, which are all part of one another, and all involved in one another."

Those who engage mindfully describe compassion as one of the key qualities which informs their actions—an outward expression exhibited toward others' suffering. When engaging with individuals, communities, and systems, compassion can be a valuable source of information. Through genuine self-observation, awareness, and a clear perspective of reality, compassion becomes not merely a way of understanding the world, but a path to full, joyful, and meaningful engagement. As we cultivate compassion, the awareness of our collective suffering is nurtured. This quality of compassion is developed as we learn ways to integrate it into our own lives—an ongoing and by no means perfect or complete practice, but a lifelong endeavor.

In the original Buddhist text, compassion was translated as both the trembling or quivering of the heart in response to pain or suffering—a feeling that emerges when witnessing another's suffering and a path to greater awareness. We are not only attending to emotional states, but witnessing the whole of the experience by embracing the full spectrum of conditions, emotions, and reactions created in any given situation. As a result, we have a benevolent response and a genuine desire to help others. The flip side of this, of course, is that we can feel overwhelmed and find ourselves drowning in these emotions—an emotional paralysis of sorts. Our actions can be stymied. We want to rescue the other, and rescue ourselves.

With mindfulness comes compassion. As we develop awareness of compassion, our ability to deal with suffering is strengthened. We can more easily witness and respond without the risk of turning away with anger, frustration, or even intolerance. This allows for greater insight into a person's responses to adversity and an open and generous heart and mind, while at the same time providing a sense of what is possible. Seen more as an attitude of altruism toward all humanity, compassion is not cultivated simply for our own sake.

Compassionate people have developed a deep knowing of their own suffering, dis-ease, and places where they get stuck in conflict and chaos, yet they do not dwell in that suffering. They can perceive the needs and interests of others and infuse that wisdom into their actions. We need to be sure that our perception of suffering is not clouded with judgment, misinformation, or denial. Having clarity of our own suffering allows us to bear witness to the suffering of others, and especially our own, even if it is difficult. As compassion grows in us, we are able to acknowledge that we are not isolated from the rest of the world, and by its very nature, compassion leads us toward wisdom and altruism.

As we cultivate compassion within ourselves, equanimity begins to emerge. Equanimity allows us to change our minds without regret. When people embody equanimity, there is a receptiveness and a giving up of imposing what "I think is best for you." With equanimity, there is balance in the midst of chaos and a sense of even-mindedness. We strive for composure, even temperedness, order, and level headedness—a poised and serene nature—a nature that is filled with abundance, exaltation, and good will. "You climb the mountain to be able to look over the whole situation, not bound by one side or the other," as Thich Nhat Hanh teaches.

This heightened insight allows us to gain a more accurate understanding of any given situation, while at the same time, guiding us towards altruistic thinking and actions. Bringing equanimity into our lives and work has great value. Without it, we are subject to different forms of discrimination and judgment that can harm the situations in which we find ourselves, as well as our relationships. We must not forget to check our motivations in order that we become keenly aware of what drives our actions, and those with whom we are engaging. We also must be able to see other perspectives and experiences with a clear and wide lens.

We are all too familiar with the fact that discrimination and judgement inevitably results in inequalities and injustice, creating lasting repercussions. In our efforts to help, we must be mindful of the inherent risk of creating an imbalance—stepping into places of power and rights, rather than acting responsibly and respectfully to help meet the needs and interests of everyone. If we fail to pay attention to potential power differences, we may become judgmental and self-righteous. If our motivations for helping others are driven by desire, anger, trauma, or self-interest, ultimately we will cause harm, so it's even more important for us to remove these obstacles and strive to create and support equity and build resilience.

Equanimity is not indifference. On the contrary, practicing the art of equanimity and cultivating compassion allows for engaging mindfully with a just and broad perspective of what has gone before, what is, and what is yet to come. It is not obtained through a simple practice, but requires us to fully embrace the things we love and also take deliberate actions to change things we know are harmful. We can learn to respond in ways that liberate us from forces designed to oppress, and at the same time know where we stand so we can take necessary actions with everyone's best interest in mind. What we see is this precious gift for recognizing and embracing possibilities and hope in others, even when that is not possible for others to see in themselves. It is this awakening of an open and good heart with the purest of motivations that helps us find the way toward right actions. These actions will manifest for the good of others and ourselves—a form of liberation without attachments.

Mindful engagement, compassionate action, and practicing the art of equanimity requires mental, emotional, and spiritual preparation and discipline. Our inner expressions of compassion become intricately linked to our actions. As we think of ways to integrate compassion and equanimity into our personal and professional lives, the intentions to act will be guided by the hope that there is some measure of goodness being bestowed on others.

STORIES THAT MATTER

Sister Simone Campbell
Cathrine Sneed
Kathy Kelly
Saraswati Gomchuyal

SISTER SIMONE CAMPBELL

As an unwavering advocate for the rights and dignity of all people, Sister Simone Campbell exemplifies what it means to work in ways that are based on religious convictions and the teachings of Jesus. Her tireless dedication to contemporary social justice issues has profound social and political impact. Sister Simone is able to amplify the voices of those who are unable to be heard by decision-makers, while her authenticity as a Catholic Sister demonstrates the depth of our understanding of compassion in action.

"Compassion, for me, is letting your heart be broken by others' stories so there's room at the table for everyone."

L et me tell you about my morning. I'm working on two issues right now—the issues at the border of the United States and Mexico, and the current situation in the Middle East. For me, when I see the situation of the unaccompanied Central American children at our border, I have a strong sense that "I need to do my part." My spiritual practice is to then listen deeply within myself to see what might emerge as to how we can be value-added in easing this crisis. My questions always are: Where can we move? What can we do? After reflection and conversation with staff, our organization decided to reach out to connect directly with what's happening on the ground, both at the border itself and in the countries from which these children are leaving. We are sharing those realities with people I think can make a difference. This includes members of Congress as well as the media.

One of the challenges with the Iraqi situation since the war is the fact that there's no attention being paid to what's going on inside the country. We had heard from the Iraqi Dominican Sisters about their plight in fleeing the extremists. Their story was horrifying. *(Note: This comment was made within a week prior to the United States 2014 military re-involvement after genocide and other atrocities in Iraq and Syria.)* I was trying to listen to that deeper call, asking myself, "What are the painful rubs we're not paying attention to?" We caused a lot of these problems in Iraq, and we're not accepting responsibility as a nation. There's a vacuum. A piece of our response here at NETWORK social justice lobby was to get the media, the White House, and the State Department involved. So I reached out to all three. Faith in action is knowing that we can do something, then listening quietly to what bubbles up.

When I listen to the urgency of people's heartbreaking stories, I cannot stay silent. I believe we are all called to let our hearts be broken, and then act on it. If everybody does one thing, then it will all get done. It's important that we not procrastinate, not hide from our own responsibility, power, and capacity. It is also important that we not feel like we have so much power that we are compelled to do something with that power in ways that may be harmful. Rather, our response should be based on the fact that people are suffering, it's wrong, and we must do something. We must act.

Being open to new possibilities or new ways forward is what I call "holding the whole of current reality." It requires mindfulness, and I do this through my meditation practice. It requires listening to the stories and not imposing my preconceptions on a situation, letting the truth of the situation emerge, and finding the connections. So, for me, being mindful is being aware that we are all connected and building on that reality. I think one of the hard parts for activists, at least in the advocacy community, is to maintain past gains while not being tied to past analysis. It's a real challenge, but I believe it's quite important. We see it in trying to maintain the safety net for people who struggle at the economic margins of our society while trying to let new models emerge. This is a delicate balance, and a place where mindfulness is so important, and where compassion plays a meaningful role.

Language is also important to mindful engagement in our lives and in our work. The way we use our words, and the ways we listen become, a way to be absolutely authentic. I had the honor of giving a nationally televised address at the 2012 Democratic National Convention. It had resonance, not so much because of the words I used, but because it was mine. I spoke to what it is that I care about—the stories of real people around the world. Even today, those who listen to what I am saying respond in ways that surprise me. To be effective, I believe you should not craft language that is disconnected from your belief. Sometimes I worry about speechwriters who simply create speeches unencumbered by the person who is going to give them. I think that language is important, but more important is its authenticity. Does it come from the inside out? Do these other qualities inform the language? Are the words, the ideas, the meaning actually mine?

We sometimes talk in catastrophic ways. When we sensationalize to get people's attention and the sky doesn't fall, we don't have any way to assess it. I really work at NETWORK to ensure that we're clear about rhetoric, about policy, and about what we see as shameless political moves on Capitol Hill. So the first step of my process is listening, and another step is being careful in our language so that we don't hype our own concerns, that we're real, and we're authentic. I talk about the 100%—"We the People"—and obviously that's the Constitution of the United States. But it's interesting to me to see advocates for social justice and reform picking up on this phrase and using it in their work and their advocacy. It's great, but I hope it's getting to their insides. I often say that what motivates me is faith, but you don't have to share my faith to share the vision. Then I say, "What holds us together as a nation is the Constitution. It's where we meet... it's We the People, it's all of us."

The work I do is about community, and it is here I find joy. Community is a reflection that I am not God. I am not judge. I do the best I can to cooperate. We're all in this together. For me, touching the pain of the world as real is the source of an active experience of hope. This hope is generated in communities where we're in this quest together. This is the reality that gives joy in the process. It's only when I think I have to do this alone that it becomes a problem and feels burdensome. My perspective of being a part of a whole keeps my work and my advocacy in perspective. When I feel it's all up to me, that's burdensome. But when I feel like we're all in this together and I'm just doing my part, then we can do this joyfully.

Compassion, for me, is letting your heart be broken by others' stories so there's room at the table for everyone. It's one thing to be in touch with your own pain and not hobbled by it, but the bigger piece is letting your heart be broken by other people's pain. There is a road we must travel, and along that road, we can become so narcissistic in our own angst that we lose sight of community. Then we are not much help to anyone. But if I hold everyone in my care, and in turn am held in his or her care, then that creates an active experience of hope. Compassion is all about this idea that our love for each other leads to the deeper truth and we are all connected. Compassion thus can reveal our best selves.

CATHRINE SNEED

The Earth can heal us only if we can touch it, work in it, and benefit from our labors and our caring. Cathrine Sneed has learned this along the way to understanding what is necessary to reform gang members, murderers, drug dealers, and car thieves. Working from a practical and realistic, yet profoundly heartfelt place, Cathrine has found the tools for engagement with results that demonstrate how a garden can become our teacher and a metaphor for creating healthy and sustainable lives and communities.

"It takes an extraordinary effort to overcome what many people have experienced, and most of us are ordinary."

I grew up wanting to be a criminal lawyer, feeling that I knew all these people that may very well eventually end up in jail. If I were a criminal lawyer, I could set them free. In 1972, I hitch-hiked from the East Coast to San Francisco. I was pregnant and felt that there must be more opportunities on the West Coast. I needed to take care of my baby and, at the same time, I truly wanted to make the world a better place. I got a house, a job, went to college, and was accepted to law school. At that time, I worked a lot with death penalty cases, but after working on four cases where one person died and the other three were as good as dead, I realized I wanted to get them out of jail and keep them out of jail. I also realized that all these things that I would try to fix and make different as a social worker didn't seem to work. The inmates I worked with didn't know what it meant to be out in a world that was different from their current experiences. They didn't have the skills to bring what I had to offer to bear in their world—a world that was chaotic, traumatizing, and unstable.

During that time I became quite ill and was in the hospital off and on for a year. While I was in the hospital, a colleague brought me John Steinbeck's novel, *The Grapes of Wrath*. They thought I'd like the book because it was about hitchhiking, since I had hitchhiked to get to California. But what I saw was these people's deep connection to the land. During their travels they couldn't connect to the land. If they had land, they could have hope. I began asking myself if working on the land could be helpful for the inmates?

Would being with the land give them hope? When I returned to work, the sheriff gave me permission to take the inmates to the land adjacent to the jail, clean it up, and see what we could do with it. So we started the garden. The inmates cleared eight acres by hand and we began planting seeds, although I had no gardening experience to speak of.

Several years ago, we were looking for more space in the San Francisco area so the former inmates could build a community garden. I called this big corporate entity and asked them if we could use one of their empty lots, clean it up, and create a big city garden. They rejected my offer. So we decided to do a project there anyway. I got them food and clothes so they could work. There were at least twelve people every day, some days fifty. In the beginning we'd climb the fence and throw out bags of garbage and then one day someone asked me, "Cathrine, why don't we cut down this fence?" Good question.... so we did. And we made a garden. Within a year it was a big garden. *The New*

York Times did an article about us and suddenly the corporation who had rejected our original offer got on board. This is where we started The Garden Project.

The garden, I believe, is a way to connect to something bigger than the self. Nature does this. And it just so happens this garden helped the inmates and former inmates learn how to work. I was traveling and panhandling all over the country, speaking at Ivy League colleges, asking for money to support the project that had gained notoriety. But people would tell me, "That project is a black hole and we're not giving money to a black hole; these people [the former inmates] should volunteer." Well, you don't volunteer when you don't have food at home. You get paid, and that's how you eat. So, we're working the land, raising crops, earning money, and doing social work because life in the outside world doesn't stop. People get shot and killed in their neighborhood the night before, and they still show up early the next day to work.

We're teaching people to work by working. It's like the plants—you have to look at the whole plant. With your hands you can make a difference. It's stewardship. Caring for things. This is our purpose, and by working in the garden, and in our larger community contracted jobs, these people are learning how to take care of themselves—and they get a check! At the same time, like mindfulness, we are supporting each other in removing obstacles—real life obstacles, and the emotional ones as well.

When I first worked with the plants, and the current and former inmates, they'd always weed out the plants and not the weeds. This is how they saw themselves—the good parts removed and only the bad parts left intact. People often don't know what's inside. They only see what's outside. I would tell them that they have to be open to being seen. The world doesn't always see you in a positive way, but so what. You need to see yourself in a positive way.

Before the gardens, they couldn't concentrate with everything that was going on in their heads—all of the questions about their pasts or their futures. Now they are really seeing what's right in front of them. The weeds keep coming, and we keep taking them out. I keep telling them, "Just weed it, then compost. Take horse manure and make soil out of it." These former inmates with unspeakable life stories say, "Look at how we can make this happen! We'll find a way out."

Working in the garden, the former inmates learned how to focus and see what's right in front of them. It is the garden that keeps them focused, and, like the plants, you have to look at the whole plant. They have learned to do this as well. It's mindful. It's important. It's beautiful. It takes an extraordinary effort to overcome what many people have experienced, and most of us are ordinary. You expect that these people who have nothing—no bootstraps, no boots—to do something different. But it's like life... you remove the weeds, keep weeding, and the garden won't change overnight. The weeds will come back. And you have to give them nourishment for strong roots. But keep working on it.

KATHY KELLY

Kathy Kelly reflects on her experiences living in war zones and promoting nonviolent resistance. Standing witness to people affected by crimes against humanity, she speaks to the violation of basic human rights and the importance of tolerance, equality, and compassion.

"Doing no harm comes from the value of hope, and if you lose it, you lose everything."

During high school I read about the Holocaust and remember thinking that I never want to be the person who is trying to be an innocent bystander while something that awful goes on. It's very challenging to live and work in ways that do no harm. We must ask ourselves daily if we are living more simply, sharing resources more radically, and preferring service to dominance in our choices and activities. We'll never be perfect.

Working alongside activists working toward a world without war has drawn me toward living in several war zones. When living in Afghanistan, Gaza, Lebanon, the West Bank, or Iraq during times of intense conflict or war, I've felt acutely aware that the present is conditioned by the past. People I live with, and with whom I've been blessed to share friendship, suffer the traumas of previous war and displacement. Many are bereaved and still grieving the loss of family members and friends. Some recall being homeless in harsh environments. Some nearly starved or froze to death. Most have been familiar with ear-splitting blasts, sickening thuds, and gut-wrenching explosions. We need communities of nonviolent resistance to defy the cultural norms that accept callous and dangerous inequities. It's interesting that some of the happiest people I know live in such communities.

I'm glad to be living in a time when people are reaching for a new vocabulary to express 'right relationship' with the world around us. Maybe we should seek adherents to "being-ism", to feeling empathy for all beings, human and animal, as well as a grateful desire to sustain planetary life. Of course, we cannot refrain from harming every being on the planet. But to whatever extent possible, living with compassionate regard for all beings seems wise and fulfilling in this precarious time when the environment has been so damaged by human overconsumption and the recklessness of human pollution and waste. Thinking about human beings, I believe those who are most in need and most impoverished should always be our top priority. How do we build empathy and compassion? The counsels of personalism are helpful. Start with personal relationships, seeking equality and learning ways to refute the idea that one person's life is more valuable than that of another person. I think it's helpful for peace activists to live alongside people trapped in war zones and in prisons so that the victims of war and of the prison-industrial complex can educate us.

After World War II, a group of young seminarians asked Albert Camus how he felt about the Catholic Church's response to the rise of Nazism. Camus said that he had longed for a loud, clear voice coming from Catholic leaders denouncing Nazism. He later realized that pronouncements had been made, but they were cloaked in the language of encyclicals and official documents which weren't widely understood by ordinary church members. Camus urged people to speak up in language that the simplest people can easily grasp. This is a responsibility that people who witness crimes hold in common. We must find creative ways to expose and denounce crimes against humanity and to nonviolently resist these crimes, believing that nonviolence can change the world. We shouldn't let inconvenience be an obstacle to acting in accord with our deepest beliefs.

Courage is the ability to control our fears. Everyone feels fear. When our fears steer our actions, we become reactive and lose our composure. Often because we feel insecure, it's difficult to regain equilibrium and control our words and actions so that we don't hurt others or violate their basic rights. One way to develop equilibrium and equanimity as members of the human family is to keep one foot firmly planted among those who are most oppressed or disadvantaged in our society and the other foot firmly planted in nonviolent resistance to oppression. I think this helps us overcome fears that governments sometimes cultivate and promote. For example, oppressive and greedy elites sometimes can control the resources of other people and profit from the weapons industry, if they can convince people that their security lies in allowing the government to make war against certain people who are considered to be enemies. The belligerent individuals in positions of power and influence will then emphasize frightening and demonic threats that the enemy poses. If citizens of one country are sufficiently frightened or feel terribly threatened, they are more likely to go along with waging war against the so-called enemy.

Racist conditions make us presume various inequalities between people. It's very difficult to break out of racist ways of thinking and perceiving. Classism, ageism, professionalism, and sexism can interfere with our ability to feel compassion and empathy. Persistent effort to overcome these "isms" is necessary. We need to encourage one another and deepen collective beliefs that we are all part of one another.

What do these wars accomplish? We lose our sense of equanimity and we find out later that we have caused havoc, destruction, suffering, and smoldering resentment amongst those who have been bereaved, maimed, displaced, and traumatized by wars. The general public in developed countries could have resisted had they been better educated about what is required to "do no harm."

I often feel hampered by language and inexperience when trying to hear what other people desperately want to tell us when they are aggrieved and enduring great suffering. We can listen better when people who are trusted interpreters accompany us. This works in personal and political life, but a deep desire to listen to the cares and concerns of others should be cultivated in every society. It's good to find ways of communicating that give people immediate involvement in empathy and problem solving and hold humility as a helpful and practical virtue.

I believe we need not choose blindness or the hatred that lets us be herded in fear. We can reach out with truth, with compassion, and with the activist courage that leaps from heart to heart, rebuilding sanity, civility, community, humanity, and resistance. We can find hope in our own active work to prove that humanity persists and that history can lean toward justice.

SARASWATI GOMCHUYAL

A spiritual teacher in India, Saraswati Gomchuyal offers his insights on compassion, equality, and right action in working with suffering and how to embrace others who are faced with great challenges. His spiritual wisdom presents a guide to approaching difficult situations, embracing the meaning of seeing ourselves in others, and the value of acting from a place of deep insight and awareness.

"We each have a unique way of moving through the world that is our own way—with our own power and our own insight."

Many people get into trouble when they think of themselves as a healer or a great spiritual teacher. This mind-set is self-love and only creates suffering for others and ourselves. The suffering of others is my suffering. This place inspires my love for others, and this love inspires my action. To truly give, one needs to step into the river of life, not just stand on the banks. Only then, can one act from a place of do no harm.

When I first began the practice of right speech, I fell into silence. I had nothing that needed to be said. I felt sated by just listening to others. After a time, many months, my words began to come out. Before this practice, I had always spoken my words as if throwing them from a whip out into the world. Now, my words were softer, kinder threads, weaving with the other. I watched as those I was having conversations with relaxed.

It is amazing how many people brace themselves in conversation with others, as if preparing for battle. When the armor is no longer needed, we can speak our truth and move along the path in a way that does no harm. Many people say, "Speak your mind." I have come to see that the mind is not the best place to speak from. It is the whole body and the mind in union with the other, which is the place of words without harm.

We are not equal in any way. We are all unique. This does not mean that we can rule over the other. No one power is bigger than the other. No insight is too small or too big. It is easy to think that everyone is like us. When we experience something, we assume that everyone else is experiencing it in the same way as we are. This is not the case.

The view of someone growing up in a desert is very different from someone growing up in a forest. One has a long view and open space into the sky, and the other the view of the density of the trees and brush. Every experience shapes us and makes us unique.

This builds our character in different ways. And yet, through quieting ourselves, we can see that we are not separate, even though we have our unique view. This is *samadhi*—the meeting of our self in others, which is also known as being in the presence of other high beings or demigods. We are all high beings. We are all awakened in our own way.

Years ago, I left the farm of my family to become a student of high spiritual knowledge. I studied yoga and meditation, only to find that I was miserable. My mind was racing, and I felt like I would explode every time I sat down in silence and followed the instructions of my teachers. I was so agitated that anyone sitting next to me could feel my inner thoughts. When my teacher approached me and asked what I was running from, I said without hesitation, "Myself!" And it was so very true. My teacher then explained that the self is actually the many. Only if I could truly embrace others, with all of their faults and gifts, could I truly be in the world from my highest self. Once I understood this, I stopped struggling and felt my own pain, desire, longing, and shame, as that of everyone in the world. It was as if I had been in a closed room without light, and suddenly, the walls fell away and I was standing in the bright sunlight.

Touching the hands of the poor, I am touching my own hands. Looking into the eyes of the small child, I am looking into my own eyes. Yes, we are not equal, but we are the same. When we touch the other, we touch ourselves. When we look into the other's eyes, we look into our own soul. This is the way of *samsara*—the cycle of life—the cycle of rebirth. Every person lives within this cycle of patterns and beliefs. The wisdom of action comes from realizing that we are not our patterns and our beliefs. We are moving all the time and shifting our view moment to moment according to what is in front of us. This is the core of right action and right speech. When we act from a belief, or something we read in a book, we create suffering. There is no set script. There is only what surrounds us and what is inside of us in the moment. Entering that reality, we see that there is no separation and we are truly all one. If we really want to help, stop thinking of ourselves as something. This way creates the act that does no harm.

THE PRACTICE OF COMPASSION

CONSIDER THIS

► Compassion can be a valuable guide as you think about how to live and work in ways that do not harm others or the planet.

► Motivations and intentions that are grounded in compassion and altruism have the power to guide your values towards actions which honor equity, inclusion and diversity.

► Be generous with your time and energy. Share your talents where they are needed as a way of contributing to the common good.

► And remember, what happens to me happens to you. And what happens to you happens to me.

NOW ASK YOURSELF

▶ What motivates me to act with compassion?

- A need to connect with others in a deeper way?

- A sense of social responsibility?

- An intention to turn my heart felt concerns into altruism—an unselfish concern for the welfare of others with an intention to act?

- Something else?

▶ What will it take for me to more fully understand my own dis-ease or suffering, the causes and conditions that contribute to suffering, and the obstacles which get in the way of my ability to be happy?

- Maybe some difficulties you faced in the past? And inability to forgive?

- Is there something happening in your life today that is causing concern or unhappiness?

- Do you have strong concerns about the chaos and disruptions going on in the world around you?

- What are you afraid of?

▶ What do I think would happen if I were to better understand the source of others' dis-ease or suffering?

- Would I be uncomfortable?

- Might I feel like I'm invading people's personal space?

- Might I think this is 'none of my business?'

- Or is it possible that empathy, sympathy, and compassion could begin to take on a different meaning for me?

▶ How can I stay balanced and undisturbed while cultivating equal consideration for all things?

- As an example: If you get agitated while in the midst of an argument with a friend, family member, or colleague, take a moment to consider everyone's best interest and proceed with caution and good will.

- Are there mindfulness practices such as meditation, prayer, gardening, walking, or something of that nature that I can practice?

- What else comes to mind that I might find helpful that could bring equanimity into focus and practice?

▶ How do I bring forward a natural unbiased openness and warmth into my daily life?

- Could I begin by being honest with myself about my own biases?

- Do I have blind spots, preconceived notions, or judgements I need to be aware of?

- Might I need to pay attention to habitual personal behaviors and feelings such as shyness, aggressiveness, or powerlessness which may affect my interactions with other people?

- Can I set an example of kindness and compassion which can serve to nurture kindness and compassion in others?

NOW PRACTICE

▶ Responding Rather than Reacting

- Notice how you either react or respond to troubling situations such as a miscommunication or 'unfairness' at home or at work. Think about a recent experience. Take a moment and jot down a few words that describe your reaction/response.

- Extend that thinking into situations that are beyond your friends, family or work. For example: local or national politics, a tense community issue, environmental disasters, social injustice, or things of that nature. Once again, take a moment and jot down a few words that describe your reaction/response.

- Do you get angry or frustrated? Do you withdraw or feel a sense of hopelessness? Do you hope that others will take care of the problem or that it's 'really not my problem'? Do you feel numb or disconnected?

- Or.... did you start thinking of ways to become involved? Were you energized to do something, small or large, to change the situation?

- Be sure to notice if there are any similarities or patterns to the ways you either responded or reacted in both cases.

▶ Understanding Your Suffering and the Suffering of Others

- Traumatic experiences, as we know, can interfere with our ability to be compassionate. As such, it is important to pay attention to our habitual responses as the response itself may cause suffering. Now bring to mind a few situations that you describe as being 'traumatic' (they don't need to be big traumas!). What was your first impulse when threatened physically or emotionally? Was it to defend yourself? Did you want to remove yourself as quickly as possible from that experience? Did you feel like hiding? Did your impulse change depending on the nature of the threat? Jot down your answers to these questions and see if there's a pattern.

- Take some time to think about a few other life experiences when you suffered (not necessarily lasting traumatic ones). Define suffering in any way you see fit.

- Just notice that experience and the thoughts and feelings that arise, without judging yourself.

- When those thoughts arise in the future, simply take three breaths, notice whatever it is that creates this dis-ease, then take three deep breaths once again. On the last exhale, recite this: "I'm letting this go".

- Practice this each time similar thoughts or feelings arise. Don't wait until you get home..... You can do this in the middle of a meeting, while watching a news segment, while in the market or the garden.

▶ Creating a Community of Practice

- Set some time aside with friends, family, or colleagues for a discussion that focuses on a subject of mutual interest related to social or political issues. (We suggest you start with social issues and move, gently, into political ones!)

- Bring your attention to the quality of compassion and the importance of equanimity before you begin.

- Ask the group how they think compassion can contribute to living and working in ways that do not harm.

THE QUALITY OF LOVE AND JOY
A SENSE OF HOPE

You don't have to make your subject
and verb agree to serve. You only need a heart
full of grace. A soul generated by love.

—MARTIN LUTHER KING, JR

L *ove and joy* is core to the practice of mindful engagement.
What we do and how we do is at the heart of compassionate
action and an expression of giving and generosity. Love and
joy help us along the path to altruism. We can remember what
we feel passionate about and what we will protect above all
else. When we allow love and joy to guide our ethics, principles,
values, and behaviors, rather than seeing them as abstract feelings, they become an expression of just and responsible action.
With a sense of hope, we have the fortitude and energy to want
to make a change. Even if it feels insurmountable, hope is what
will help us stay motivated and continue with our lives and our
work. Love, joy, and a sense of hope can help sustain us.

When inspired by deep acts of love and energized by joy, we
are able to respond even in the face of daunting adversity and
take actions that are born from the depths of what it is to be
human. The love that motivated the civil rights movement,
for example, was redemptive love from the Greek word *agape*,
considered to be the highest form of love known to humanity.
Agape is a kind of love that is committed to the well-being of
others. Martin Luther King Jr. embraced agape as good will for

the common good based on the mutual interests that derive from the interrelatedness of all people. Solidarity, mutuality and interconnectedness were major guiding principles in King's activism and leadership upholding that "Nonviolence is a weapon fabricated of love. It is a sword that heals."

Out of love, the willingness to act selflessly arises naturally. Through the concept of *satyagraha*, Gandhi infused love into politics. Satyagraha is love-force or truth-force which the American Civil Rights movement revised into soul-force. Truth (satya) implies love, and firmness (agraha) engenders and therefore serves as a synonym for force. "I thus began to call the Indian movement Satyagraha, that is to say, the force which is born of truth and love or non-violence, and gave up the use of the phrase 'passive resistance'. . ." wrote Gandhi. Doing something out of love, from a place of wanting to help, can offer us the profound experience of deep compassion and benevolence for those who are suffering. Cultivating this kind of love not only benefits others but creates a life that brings a sense of meaning and purpose. Some people become heroes through this type of love while others may find small ways to give to those who are in need. Even bringing a wish of good will to people we dislike and those we consider our enemies, can help cultivate a positive outcome. It is not that we are condoning our enemies' plans to harm others, but instead we are imagining they will give up their hatred, cruelty, and indifference and begin to care for the happiness of others.

Forgetting what we love and abandoning that which is closest to us is the beginning of succumbing to things that may not support our sensibilities or feed our souls. At that point, we may become dispirited. When we fail to take actions related to the things we care about, we lose the courage to protect ourselves and the things we hold dear and give us joy. This is why we must resist any effort by outside forces to isolate people by suppressing connection, community, culture, and the like. "Joy doesn't betray but sustains activism," says writer, historian, and activist Rebecca Solnit. "And when you face a politics that aspires to make you fearful, alienated and isolated, joy is a fine act of insurrection."

Lily Yeh is an international artist dedicated to bringing art and creativity into places that are broken—places where there is minimal action and little hope for the future. She has worked with hundreds of children and families to transform bleak villages into places of beauty and joy. "We are creating an art form that comes from the heart and reflects the pain and sorrow of people's lives. It also expresses joy, beauty and love. This process lays the foundation for building a genuine community in which people are reconnected with their families, sustained by meaningful work, nurtured by the care of each other, and will together raise and educate their children. We witness social change in action. Our joy is rooted in the depth of our tragedy, our challenges, and our difficulties. We don't have to save the world, we just have to start with step one, with small things— start with small things, but with big love."

Integrating love and joy, with a sense of hope into our lives allows us to expand and extend our experiences of heightened well-being and increased satisfaction. Engaging in this way can fine-tune our perceptions, purpose and unique passions, values and strengths. No matter what form love and joy come in, it can help us overcome obstacles and change our way of being in 'right relationship' with ourselves, others, and the world. "Work is love made visible. If you cannot work with love but only with distaste, it is better that you should leave your work and sit at the gate of the temple and take alms of those who work with joy," wrote Khalil Gibran. The world cannot change on its own. The power of human love and joy, leading to collective action, carries all the power we need to create a better future.

STORIES THAT MATTER

Daniel Kaniela Akaka, Jr.
Sarah James
Yumi Kikuchi Morita

DANIEL KANIELA AKAKA, JR.

The spiritual nature of mindful engagement and r esponsibility to all things is captured in the stories of Danny Akaka, artist, historian, and indigenous Hawai'ian spiritual teacher. His gift of "talk story" in the Hawai'ian tradition paints a landscape of deep connections to our ancestors, our families, the communities in which we live, and the spirit of the land and sea. Danny's belief in the value of harmony, unity, and diversity as a foundation for our work is communicated in such a way that we are able to see the joy, beauty, and aloha in all things.

"In giving the canoe spirit and intelligence, it's not only your inner feelings that guide you, it's the feelings of the canoe itself that will guide you."

Kuleana is a word used frequently in Hawai'i. We grew up knowing *kuleana* as a responsibility—a responsibility we carry from before we come into this world. Everyone is born with a *kuleana* to fulfill. We may not understand that *kuleana* until much later in our life. Sometimes that *kuleana* may not be fulfilled in this lifetime, and it will carry on until it can be fulfilled. *Kuleana* is connected to love—*aloha*—and is that thing that brings together all that has been separated. 'Aloha' means mutual regard and affection and extends warmth in caring with no obligation in return. *Alo* means 'face to face' and *Ha* means 'breath of life' and is the essence of relationships in which each person is important to every other person for collective existence. 'Aloha' is to hear what is not said, to see what cannot be seen and to know the unknowable. In the Hawai'ians' profound understanding of Spirit and nature, they know that everything is interconnected.

There are five words that represent the Hawaiian Aloha: Akahai, meaning kindness, to be expressed with tenderness; Lōkahi, meaning unity, to be expressed with harmony; 'Olu'olu, meaning agreeable, to be expressed with pleasantness; Ha'a-ha'a, meaning humility, to be expressed with modesty; and Ahonui, meaning patience, to be expressed with perseverance. Hawai'ians gave some four hundred thousand names to all things in life—including fishing, farming, and taking stones to make the temples. These names represent the compatibility of humans with each other, the 'ohana, and with all of nature, the 'aina. The secret and beauty of Hawai'i is the human spirit, which is pono—in right balance.

In my life, I have blessed and chosen names for a number of Hawai'ian canoes. In blessing the canoe you, in essence, give it a spirit, a name, and, at the very end, you ask the question, "Is this canoe a good canoe?" In giving the canoe spirit and intelligence, it's not only your inner feelings that guide you, it's also the feelings of the canoe itself that will guide you. Everyone is on their personal canoe, and you have to allow it to go on its own. You go with the flow. The flow includes all things sent by the ancestors and the gods, the winds and the currents.

In the midst of life's challenges and obstacles, I've come to understand that you can meet many people on this journey. You may meet people from different cultures, different languages, but find you are all on the same path. There are really no accidents in the places you go and the people that you meet. As time goes on it becomes more apparent as to how things simply come together; it happens at moments that you least expect and that are mostly unplanned.

Things happen for a reason, and my meeting the Dalai Lama confirms my belief in this concept. His Holiness the 14th Dalai Lama visited Maui, Hawai'i. Prior to the larger community and international gathering with the Dalai Lama, there was a planned meeting with a representative group of eight native Hawai'ians. In the hour we spent with him, his nature and character were like that of a young child—eager to learn, very playful, and light-hearted. He had many questions for us. At the very end of our time with him, he thanked us and asked for a closing prayer. We made a circle and held hands. I happened to be right next to him. We were silent. To my surprise, the Dalai Lama turned to me and asked if I'd lead the prayer. I had to think quickly and pray for the words to come. What do you say in a prayer in front of the Dalai Lama? So I started the prayer in Hawai'ian. Mine was a prayer of thanksgiving—for the Dalai Lama and what he brings to the world, his sense of enlightenment, for our *kupunas* (elder and ancestral teachers), our island home that gives us strength and *mana* (spiritual quality) to do what we need to do. As I came to the closing, the words from one of my uncle's famous sermons came to me.

The story goes like this: The four strings of the ukulele are tuned in different keys, and the strings represent all people, cultures, colors, and diversity in the world. Although the strings are tuned differently, when played together, they make a beautiful tune. My uncle would strum the ukulele during his sermons, and then he would slack one of the strings and strum. It was not a pleasing sound because one string throws off all the rest. Yet when you have the hands of God to retune the strings to the pitch it should be, and you strum the ukulele, it restores the harmony. So he would end his sermon by saying, "Unity is diversity in harmony." And that's how I ended the prayer.

As the Dalai Lama was whisked off to greet the large crowd of people waiting for him, one of the camera men came to me and said, "I just need to share with you that when you ended the prayer, you should have seen the expression on the Dalai Lama's face. He looked up as if there was this great gift bestowed upon him." We may not be the same, but we must come together in harmony. We need to be tuned back to where we were meant to be.

As I see the way the world is going, all I can think is, we have to re-tune that string. We need to instill the spirit of aloha and help that one string to retune: to bring it back to harmony. This is our *kuleana*.

SARAH JAMES

Since time immemorial the Gwich'in, also known as the Caribou People, have lived in the area of northeast Alaska and Northwest Canada. The Gwich'in Nation holds the belief that there is no separation between humans and the earth and that all living things are profoundly connected. Sarah James, Gwich'in elder, shares her wisdom of promoting the protection of the environment through honoring the deep spiritual roots and stories of her people.

"If one tears apart the fabric of life, we have only pieces with torn edges that cannot be put back together."

The way my people learned to speak is by listening to the earth and learning the language of the rivers. This is how my people survive-by hearing what is around us, understanding the language of the seasons, the rain, and the plants growing, and what the caribou are saying. This is how we listen and come to know the language of all things, including the wind, the ice and snow, the polar bear, the arctic owl, the wolves, the snow goose, the sun, the moon, and the stars. This language holds the threads that connect the earth, the universe, and all living things that make up our world. Without this language, there can be no life.

Everything has its own way of life. We are whole people who work from the place of the circle. We are one with the universe. We understand from our connection to the earth that without the sun there wouldn't be life; without the clouds there wouldn't be rain. If one tears apart the fabric of life, we have only pieces with torn edges that cannot be put back together. It is the way of my people to create the thread to mend the damage done and to bring it back into balance. We need to believe in this, or life as we know it will fall apart. The Gwich'in have knowledge and wisdom that cannot be taken away from us. One elder told me that when the non-Indian came, they thought we would give up our wisdom, but we did not. That is what guides us today.I am one of the messengers chosen to speak the truth and tell the story of the Gwich'in people. We are also known as one of the "Caribou People" of Alaska. Arctic village is located 110 miles northeast of the Arctic Circle. It's one of the most isolated places in the United States, and we're the most northern Indian village in the United States. There is no running water and there is no road leading to our village. The only way to get there is by air. The Gwich'in are spread out far and wide, living in fifteen different villages in Mackenzie Delta, in Northwest Territories, Northern Yukon Territory in Canada, and Northeast Alaska.

We don't have luxuries that some people have in the land of the plenty. We are long-distance people living in Arctic inland, semi-desert conditions, many miles from the sea. Everyone living this way needs to know how to survive because we live in a very harsh environment. We know that the land is important to us and, in order for the land to take care of us, we need to take care of it. I have been told since I was small to be aware of the environment around me, and I will die with that awareness. My people practice this awareness from the time we are born to the time we die.

The survival of Gwich'in is totally dependent on the earth. The elements demand that we are skilled in hunting and listening to all of the living things around us. Any change could be critical to our survival. In order to live in this environment, we must watch out for anything unusual about the sun, the sky, or the weather, because if it is not healthy, it could kill us. We now live in two worlds. One is living with this dependence on our knowledge of the earth, and the other is living in cabins with electricity. Today, even with electricity, we still go out and gather food and hunt the caribou. Seventy-five percent of our diet is wild meat, and most of it comes from the Porcupine River caribou herd.

The Porcupine River caribou migrate thousands of miles each year. When April comes around, they head up north to the coastal plain of the Arctic National Wildlife Refuge to have their calves. This is seventy-five miles from our village. When my people were nomadic, we never went to that place, because we considered it to be sacred to the Porcupine caribou, and it has been that way for thousands of years. If the caribou calving and nursery grounds were ever harmed, it would be the end of the Gwich'in way of life.

The Arctic National Wildlife Refuge is one of North America's last great wilderness areas. Often it is called the "American Serengeti." It is a rich land full of some of the most pristine ecosystems on earth and home to more than two hundred bird species, forty-two species of fish, and mammals including polar bears, wolverines, moose, and Dall sheep. Migratory birds and ducks fly in from all over the world to nest. Bears, wolves, and other animals raise their young on the coastal plain. It's a special time for these animals to be safe and comfortable. This is why we call it a birthplace. A place that is overpowered with actions that threaten the health of the Earth, such as oil drilling, are not safe for a mother and young while they are nursing. The place needs to be peaceful and close to the natural environment and natural rhythms. Any birthplace should be sacred. In my language we say *'Izhak Gwats'an Gwandaii Goodlit*, which means "the sacred place where life begins." The Gwich'in have always protected our land and the caribou, and it is our way of life to do so. All of my actions come from the fact that our life depends on protecting because it is about our basic survival. We believe everything is related and it's our responsibility to keep things in balance.

Back in 1988, the United States government proposed to do oil drilling in the Arctic National Wildlife Refuge. The area proposed for drilling was 1.5 million acres and in the biological heart of the entire 19 million-acre refuge. The United States government set aside the coastal plain and left it up to Congress to either permanently protect it or open it up for oil development. The threat of oil drilling was very alarming to my people. The Gwich'in Nation depends on caribou for our food.

Just as the legendary buffalo herds were vital to Plains Indians, the caribou is the food, language, stories, dances, and songs of the Gwich'in Nation. Any industrial development would interrupt the life cycle of the Porcupine River caribou that has been the foundation of Gwich'in culture and subsistence for twenty-thousand years. Global warming has already disturbed the ecosystems of the refuge. The permafrost on the tundra is showing signs of melting, affecting food supply and migration patterns of Arctic wildlife, including the caribou.

In June 1988, the elders called a gathering in Arctic village. This was the first such gathering in 150 years, with fifteen chiefs, fifteen elders, and fifteen youth representing all the Gwich'in villages. Our coming together was like the rebirth of the nation. The elders took over the meeting and tore up the written agenda and said we had to speak our native language. Then the chiefs brought out a talking stick made of wood and said, "This is what we are going to use to talk, and there will be no written notes. We are making history and it is important this is happening."

The leaders went to the top of a hill where they created a resolution and then took it back to the elders and convinced them to pass it. The resolution was to protect the Porcupine River caribou calving ground and the Gwich'in way of life. It was decided that in order for the resolution to work, the elders had to choose people to go out and speak to the world in a good way. It was hard for the elders to make the decision for people to go out into the world and tell our story because they knew that our tribe would become known throughout the world and people would want to come to our village. This would pose yet another threat to our way of life. They formed the Gwich'in Steering Committee and chose four people from Canada and four from the United States to represent the resolution. I was one of the people chosen.

I felt honored because I knew protecting the land and my people was a deeply held responsibility I had grown up with and a major part of my life. Traveling all over the United States, I addressed environmental groups, churches, and university students. Over the years, I have spoken at the United States Congress and the United Nations. I have met with influential people such as Jimmy Carter, Hillary Clinton, and Robert Redford. It has been crucial that I tell the story of the Gwich'in to try and help others understand how critical it is to my people and other tribes to not have oil development on our land.

I have been in many situations where I was yelled at, including by politicians in Washington, D.C. Once I stood in front of a United States Senator who yelled at me for twenty minutes. As I listened to him, I stood there watching his anger and his pain. I could just watch without reacting because I know my place and where I come from. After he stopped yelling, there was a long silence between us. He looked at me and asked, "Aren't you going to respond?" I told him that in my family, we speak the language of living things and he was speaking as an angry man who didn't understand the voices of the living. He was speaking to the one, not the whole. When I said this, he looked shocked and his eyes welled up with tears. I knew that his heart had heard my words.

From the place of our ancestors, we made a decision about the gas and oil development to protect the caribou and our way of life. This is why we remain committed to this fight, because it was our decision that comes from our deep connection to the land and our roots. This way of working unifies us and the wisdom we have will keep coming back through dreams and visions and by exercising our tribal power.

When the elders gave us the direction to go out into the world and educate the people, we were told to do it in a good way and not compromise. I learned growing up that you respect your neighbors and this is what I use throughout the country when I speak and do community outreach. So far there has been no drilling and it is still protected. We continue our work for permanent protection in the Arctic National Wildlife Refuge.

The Creator put us here to take care of this part of the world and we are not going anywhere else. In my tribe when we gather and hold the talking stick, we are talking for the Earth.

We know the right thing to do is to stand up and speak out for protecting the environment. In Western culture "you" means an individual, separate from others. When I speak in front of Congress and other groups, I speak for those things that cannot speak for themselves.

Gwich'in were born with the knowledge that everything is connected and that we are the earth itself. The earth is our life. We are trying to use the good tools from the Western world and use our way of life at the same time. This is very difficult, but necessary. There are many people who talk about peace, but we will never have peace unless we clean up our actions and clean up the earth. To do this in a good way, we need to promote understanding and a deep sense of responsibility.

YUMI KIKUCHI MORITA

Escaping from the Fukushima nuclear accident in March 11, 2011, Yumi shares her personal story of what it means to work from a place of compassion with those who are experiencing the ongoing outfall from radiation exposure. She speaks about how we can address the suffering and fear of people traumatized by environmental disasters.

"This way of being, of working, is a lifelong practice of keeping your mind and heart flexible so you can continue to deepen your insight."

I have a dream that humans are evolving to become more responsible stewards of the planet and that we will not rely on nuclear power plants. We will have more safe energy that is not creating a problem for future generations. I see this as a turning point for humanity to wake up and live more carefully and consciously with the planet and with each other. Sixty-five years ago, Japanese and Americans were killing each other. But we've come this far. We're not killing each other now. We are helping. Humans are born open and pure. We have the capability to help each other, support each other, and love each other.

My work is all about hope. I don't actually know what is going to happen in Fukushima, but I am empowering the people and working to help the children from Fukushima be messengers for the future of how to protect the planet and how to live in the world in a way that protects rather than harms.

Through a difficult divorce from my first husband, I lost the custody of my two young children, which is customary in my country. It was the most painful experience in my life. When the United States started bombing Afghanistan and when 9/11 happened, I could feel the grief of the mothers and their children, and immediately I was full of compassion because of my own personal experience. My loss made my heart bigger. I was an activist before, but that pain created an even deeper compassion. When the nuclear accident happened in Fukushima in 2011, my second husband and I, with our two children, fled to Okinawa to protect our family from the radiation. When we got to Okinawa, we worked day and night to get pregnant women and children out of Fukushima.

During the first two months, many people living in Fukushima were exposed to high levels of radiation, and mothers are now very concerned as thyroid cancer continues to increase in babies and young children. They were torn to make a decision whether to leave the area or not, even though they knew the radiation levels were extremely high. Officials have told them that it is safe for children to be outside for only one hour a day. For many mothers, their husbands' jobs are in Fukushima. Imagine living in a place that you know is poisoning your children but you cannot leave. Everyone is suffering in this, because if you stay, you are risking the lives of your children, and if you leave, you are betraying the family.

I am doing my best to inform people about the health consequences of living in Fukushima. In order to help, my husband and I have created Fukushima Kids on the island of Hawai'i so that families and their children have a refuge to come to and take a break from the radiation exposure. The mothers are so grateful when they come to Hawai'i to visit. They can have their children touch the water and work in the vegetable garden, even walk outside, without living in constant fear of radiation poisoning. When I see these mothers with their children come over from Japan, not wanting to go back because they want to protect their children, it is very hard for me. I feel their struggle and their pain. This is what compassion is—feeling the pain of another in your own heart. My work in the world comes from this place.

I have found that it is important to deeply listen to the person in front of me. To do this I must be in the moment. I avoid putting a label on the person, and I don't victimize them. It would be easy for me to think that because they are from Fukushima, they need something specific because they have experienced a traumatic event. However, everyone is different in how they respond to trauma. When people are lumped together into the same category, it minimizes their own power to heal.

We can learn and listen to others speak about their suffering. When a mother cries and says to me, "What do I do to keep my baby safe from radiation when I go back to Fukushima? How will my child survive?" it is very hard for me to hear this question. The reality of how to keep her baby safe is to stay indoors all day and all night. Things we have always believed to be safe for our children become dangerous, such as playing in the park or working in the garden. She cannot take her baby outside because radiation clings to the pollen and dust. It is everywhere in the soil. Witnessing her suffering without judging it, or adding in my own story, becomes the medicine for healing. Sometimes we just need to let others know that we are really seeing them and acknowledge that they have a story that is hard. When this happens, they no longer have to cling to their story, and they can move forward. It is bringing something hidden into the light.

One of the things that I do to connect with another person is recognize my own deep emotion and know what I really want in the moment. What I really want in my work is connection, love, and wellbeing for Fukushima children. When I contact this place in myself, I can speak to the universal human needs and what we all share, desire, and hope for. When I have deep sadness, I remember this place of love, trust, connection, and wellbeing. It helps me rebalance myself so I can really listen to someone speak about their pain. If something someone does or says shakes my heart, I translate that into what they are really wanting—a yearning for something bigger, such as truth, authenticity, justice, or peace. This helps me stay focused on what I genuinely want to offer to them in the moment. This way of being, of working, is a lifelong practice of keeping your mind and heart flexible so you can continue to deepen your insight and love for your work.

THE PRACTICE OF LOVE AND JOY

CONSIDER THIS

► Loving what you do, with joyful enthusiasm, can truly sustain you.

► Practice being in the world in a way that is 'love made visible'.

► Be mindful of what it is that you feel passionate about and what you will protect above all else.

► And remember to do what you truly love, and do it often.

NOW ASK YOURSELF

▶ What does it mean for me to love what I do and commit to doing what I love?

- Do I love what I do? If yes, how can I sustain that? If not, how can I find a way to make my relationship to what I do more joyful and happy?

- What does it feel like when I really love what I do?

- Have I forgotten what I love and hold dear? If so, why?

▶ How does love and joy play a role in supporting my actions for the common good?

- Other than my romantic life, in what ways have love and joy played a role in supporting what I choose to do in my work, in my community, with my friends or family, or something else?

- What does this phrase mean to me, 'work is love made visible'?

- How does that phrase relate to my work in the world?

NOW PRACTICE

▶ Acting from a Place of Love and Joy

- Identify what it is that gives your life meaning and purpose. Now ask yourself if love and joy play any part in this meaning-making.

- Make a list of at least three experiences in your community (i.e. relationships, workplaces, volunteerism) where you feel cared for and where you have felt a sense of joy.

Can you bring this feeling out into the world for the benefit of others and if so, how? If not, why not?

- Think about a time you lacked the ability to act from a place of love and joy. What was the outcome? Did you have less energy, less enthusiasm, less connection to what you were doing or who you were interacting with?

- How can you bring more love and joy into your everyday life, the work you do, and the changes you'd like to see happen? Make a list of ways you can do this from small to bigger actions. Consider ways you might implement.

- Spend some quiet time to reflect on the things you hold dear. For example: friends, family, the nature of your work, the environment, your community. What is it about these that you value most?

▶ Creating a Community of Practice

- Set some time aside with friends, family, or colleagues for a discussion that focuses on a subject of mutual interest related to social or political issues. (We suggest you start with social issues and move, gently, into political ones!)

- Bring your attention to the quality of love and joy before you begin.

- Ask the group how they think love and joy can contribute to living and working in ways that do not harm.

AUTHORS' BIOGRAPHY

Wendy Wood, PhD and Thaïs Mazur, PhD, co-founders of The Karuna Center for Mindful Engagement, are human scientists, educators, community activists, authors, and peacebuilders. Working internationally, they have led efforts on social, environmental, economic, and occupational justice; integrative medicine; conflict transformation; trauma and peacebuilding; art for social change; violence prevention and intervention; and social systems reform. Wendy and Thaïs are native Californians and have lived and worked in rural and urban communities throughout the world.

Learn more: www.thekarunacenter.org

CONTRIBUTORS' BIOGRAPHIES

Daniel Kaniela Akaka, Jr. is a storyteller in the ancient Hawai'ian tradition. He knew the Hawai'ian coastline long before there were resorts brimming with tourists. Diplomacy runs deep in Akaka's family. His father was a United States Senator and his uncle coined the term the "Aloha Spirit", living in right balance with nature. Akaka brings to life the legacy of Hawai'i through story to keep the spirit alive and thriving. He and his wife were part of the Hawai'ian renaissance, bringing back the practices and reclaiming the legacy of the Hawai'ian people.

Jeannette Armstrong, PhD is Syilx Okanagan, a fluent speaker of Nsyilxcn, and a traditional knowledge keeper of the Okanagan Nation, and a founder of En'owkin, the Syilx knowledge revitalization institution of higher learning. She currently holds the Canada Research Chair in Okanagan Indigenous Knowledge and Philosophy at UBC Okanagan. She has a PhD in Environmental Ethics and Syilx Indigenous Literatures, and is the recipient of the EcoTrust Buffett Award for Indigenous Leadership. She is an author and Indigenous activist who has published works including literary titles and academic writing on a wide variety of Indigenous issues. Jeannette currently serves on Canada's Traditional Knowledge Subcommittee of the Committee on the Status of Endangered Wildlife in Canada.

Sister Simone Campbell joined the Sisters of Social Service, an international Roman Catholic Religious congregation rooted in the Benedictine tradition, in 1964, and took her final vows in 1973. She received a bachelor's degree from Mount St. Mary's College and a Juris Doctor from the University of California, Davis. After graduating from law school, Sister Simone founded the Community Law Center in Oakland, California, serving for 18 years as its lead attorney. She practiced family law and advocated for people in poverty. Between 1995 and 2000, she was the General Director of her religious institute and oversaw its activities in the United States, Mexico, Taiwan and the Philippines. Sister Simone Campbell recently retired as the founder and Executive Director of NETWORK, a national Catholic social justice lobby. In March 2010, as the United States Congress debated reforms to health care, known as the Patient Protection and Affordable Care Act, she wrote the "nuns' letter" supporting the reforms and asked leaders of Catholic Sisters to sign it. The letter, signed by 59 Sisters, was sent to all members of Congress and contributed to the momentum in favor of the legislation. Sister Simone gave a major address at the Democratic National Convention held in September 2012 and in June 2020. She leads NETWORK's "Nuns on the Bus" campaign. In 2012, the first year of the campaign, the Nuns on the Bus traveled thousands of miles to draw attention to Catholic Sisters' work in low-income communities and to protest federal budget cuts to programs that serve human needs. Subsequent "Nuns on the Bus" journeys focused on immigration reform, Medicaid expansion, and the importance of voting. In honor of her advocacy work, she was the 2014 recipient of the Pacem in Terris Peace and Freedom award. Sister Simone Campbell lives in Washington, D.C. www.networklobby.org

Kenneth Cloke, JD, PhD is Director of the Center for Dispute Resolution. As an internationally known mediator and arbitrator, Ken specializes in resolving complex multi-party conflicts which include: community, family, grievance and workplace disputes, collective bargaining negotiations, organizational conflicts, sexual harassment and discrimination lawsuits, and public policy disputes. He also provides services in designing conflict resolution systems for organizations. He is a nationally recognized speaker and author of many books and journal articles, as well as an attorney, coach, consultant, and trainer. He received his B.A. from the University of California, Berkeley; J.D. from UC Berkeley's Boalt Law School; PhD from UCLA; LLM from UCLA Law School; and did postdoctoral work at Yale University School of Law. He is a graduate of the National Judicial College. In 2009, Ken co-founded Mediators Beyond Borders International, a group whose mission is to bring conflict resolution and mediation skills to communities around the globe. Ken is a prolific author whose books include *Mediating Dangerously*; *The Crossroads of Conflict*; *Conflict Revolution: Mediating Evil*; *War, Injustice and Terrorism*; and *The Dance of Opposites*. Kenneth Cloke lives in Southern California. www.kennethcloke.com

Joan Goldsmith, PhD is an organizational consultant and educator, specializing in leadership development, organizational change, conflict resolution, team building, and information systems. From 1985 to 1990, as a principal with CSC Index, she directed Index China, developing business bridges between the United States and China, and assisted Fortune 100 clients in business reengineering, change management, and human resource development. She is coauthor with Warren Bennis of *Learning to Lead: A Workbook on Becoming a Leader* and coauthor with Kenneth Cloke of *Mediating Dangerously* and *Resolving Conflicts at Work*. Joan is founder of the national program for women in leadership development, Women Leaders: Creating Ourselves at the Crossroads. She has been a family therapist and serves on the Boards of Directors of three national organizations. She was an associate of the Synergos Institute building collaborative partnerships to end poverty in the Southern hemispheres and has been an adviser in organizational development and school reform to school districts in major cities. She is cofounder of Mediators Beyond Borders International, Cambridge College, and a former member of the faculties of Harvard University, UCLA, Antioch University, Southern Methodist University, and Pepperdine University Law School, Straus Institute. She holds a doctorate in Humane Letters. Joan Goldsmith lives in Southern California.

Saraswati Gomchuyal was born in 1943 in Nagaland, India and has been a teacher and practitioner of Vedanta meditation and Ashtanga Vinyasa yoga since he was twelve years old. Saraswati believes that the practice of doing no harm begins with recognizing that suffering is not an individual experience, but a reflection of the world at large. Devoting himself to easing the hardship of poverty, he has applied this belief and is a foremost advocate for the rights of prisoners, women, and children. Saraswati Gomchuyal lives in India.

Sarah James is a Neets'aii Gwich'in Indian from Arctic village Alaska. She grew up in the traditional way of the Gwich'in. Chosen to represent her people, Sarah is a tribal elder who travels throughout the world telling the story of her people and speaking out against oil drilling in the Arctic National Wildlife Refuge and for permanent protection of 'Izhik Gwats'an Gwandaii Goodlit. Sarah is chairperson of the Gwich'in Steering Committee. She has educated the Gwich'in people about bioaccumulation of persistent organic pollutants, especially in cold Arctic regions. A keynote speaker at conferences around the world, Sarah has given testimony to both the U.S. Senate and House of Representatives. She is working to set up a community radio station in Arctic Village that would promote her people's language and culture. Sarah sits on the board of the International

Indian Treaty Council, is a member of the Indigenous People Subcommittee of the United States Environmental Protection Agency's National Environmental Justice Advisory Council, and a special advisor to the Yukon River Inter-Tribal Watershed Council. Sarah James lives in Arctic Village.

Kathy Kelly is a co-coordinator of Voices for Creative Nonviolence, a campaign to end U.S. military and economic warfare. Kathy and her companions believe that nonviolence entails simplicity, service, sharing of resources, and nonviolent direct action in resistance to war and oppression. In 1996, Kathy helped found Voices in the Wilderness, a group dedicated to witnessing the suffering that the United States and United Nations imposed sanctions inflicted on people in Iraq, especially the children. They defied the sanctions by bringing medicines to children and families in Iraq. From 1996–2003, Voices activists formed seventy delegations that openly defied economic sanctions by bringing medicines to children and families in Iraq. Kathy and her companions lived in Baghdad throughout the 2003 "Shock and Awe" bombing. During recent trips to Afghanistan, Kathy Kelly, as an invited guest of the Afghan Peace volunteers, has lived alongside ordinary Afghan people in a working-class neighborhood in Kabul. She and her companions in Voices for Creative Nonviolence believe that "where you stand determines what you see." Kathy graduated from the Chicago Theological Seminary and has been an advocate for antipoverty and nonviolence throughout the world. More information is available at www.vcnv.org.

Ibu Robin Lim, CPM is a midwife and founder of Bumi Sehat, a nonprofit organization in Indonesia. Along with a group of team members, Ibu Robin runs medical relief and childbirth clinics in Bali, Aceh (post tsunami), and Dulag, Philippines (in the aftermath of the superstorm Typhoon Haiyan). The seed of the Birthkeeper, for Ibu Robin, was planted by her Filipino grandmother, who was a Hilot traditional healer. Her inspiration is her family. In 2006, the Alexander Langer Foundation honored Ibu Robin in the Italian Parliament. In 2011, Ibu Robin was chosen CNN Hero of the Year. This gave midwife-to-mother care a broader, popular platform worldwide. In 2012, The Association for Prenatal and Perinatal Psychology and Health gave Ibu Robin the Jeannine Parvati BirthKeeper of the Year award. Robin has published many books including: *After the Baby's Birth*; *Wellness for Mothers*; *Eating for Two: Recipes for Pregnant and Breast-feeding Women*; *Placenta–the Forgotten Chakra*; *Eat Pray Doula*; *Butterfly People*; *The Geometry of Splitting Souls* (poetry), and many more. In 2009, Robin's daughter, Déjà Bernhardt, released two award winning films, *Guerrilla Midwife* and *Tsunami Notebook* documenting Lim's work and the essential importance of gentle birth for a more peaceful planet. To see the work of Ibu Robin: www.bumisehatfoundation.org

Yumi Kikuchi Morita is a published author and translator of books and films. She was born and raised in Tokyo. After being a writer and a bond trader, she chose to work solving environmental problems. She is a founding member of several NGOs Since she moved to the Kamogawa countryside of Chiba, she started sustainable living with her husband Gen Morita. Along with their children, they grew most of what they ate organically. The day immediately following the Fukushima Daiichi Nuclear Power Plant disaster, they left their organic farm in Kamogawa and eventually moved to Kona, Hawai'i. She and her husband practice harmonics healing together, sharing Japanese ancient natural healing methods with the community. Their volunteer mission, Fukushima kids Hawai'i, has been bringing children from Fukushima to Kona to help their immune systems recover from radiation exposure. Yumi Kukuchi Morita lives with her family in Hawai'i. www.fukushimakidsHawai'i.com

Mayumi Oda was born in a suburb of Tokyo in 1941. Mayumi knows of the sufferings of war, coupled with a passionate commitment to the expression of joy. An internationally recognized artist, her bold contemporary imagery has been identified with the work of Matisse. She has had many one-woman exhibits in Japan, Europe, and the U.S., and her work is in the permanent collections of the Museum of Modern Art in New York, the Museum of Fine Arts in Boston, and the Library of Congress. In addition to her work as an artist, Mayumi has spent many years of her life as a global activist, participating in antinuclear campaigns worldwide. She founded Plutonium Free Future in 1992. On behalf of her organization, Mayumi lectured and held workshops on nuclear patriarchy to solar communities at the United Nations' NGO Forum and the Women of Vision Conference in Washington, DC. In 1999, she launched the World Atomic Safety Holiday (WASH) Campaign and is currently working to raise awareness among the citizens of Hawai'i about the use of depleted uranium at the Pohakuloa military base. Mayumi Oda lives in Hawai'i. www.mayumioda.net

Bruce D. Perry, MD, PhD is the senior fellow of The Child Trauma Academy, a nonprofit organization based in Houston, Texas, and adjunct professor in the Department of Psychiatry and Behavioral Sciences at the Feinberg School of Medicine at Northwestern University in Chicago. He serves as the inaugural senior fellow of the Berry Street Childhood Institute, an Australian based center of excellence focusing on the translation of theory into practice to improve the lives of children (www. berrystreet.org.au). Dr. Perry is the author, with Maia Szalavitz, of *The Boy Who Was Raised as a Dog*, a bestselling book based on his work with maltreated children and *Born for Love: Why Empathy Is Essential and Endangered.* Over the last thirty years, Dr. Perry has been an active teacher, clinician, and researcher in children's mental health and neurosciences, holding a variety of academic positions. Bruce Perry lives in Texas. www.childtrauma.org

Richard Reoch a lifelong Buddhist, has devoted himself to peace, the defense of human rights, conflict resolution, intercultural communications and the protection of the environment. Born in Canada, he moved to England in 1971 to join the headquarters of Amnesty International, where he was the global media chief and appeared worldwide on TV, radio, and in the press. Reoch currently is the chair of the International Working Group on Sri Lanka, a network of diplomats and experts supporting the peace process on that war-torn island. He is the author of *Combating Torture*, the official field manual of the fifty-five nation Organization for Security and Cooperation in Europe. He served as a consultant on torture prevention with the Indian National Human Rights Commission. He is also an adviser to human rights groups on both sides of the border in Ireland. In the early 1990s, Reoch was invited by the musician/activist Sting to help lead the Rainforest Foundation, dedicated to the preservation of the rainforests and their peoples. He continues to serve as a trustee of its U.K. foundation. In 2002, Sakyong Mipham Rinpoche, head of the Shambhala Mandala, a worldwide contemplative community dedicated to the creation of Enlightened Society, appointed Reoch to the position of president. Reoch is also the author of *To Die Well: A Holistic Approach for the Dying and Their Caregivers.* Richard Reoch lives in Europe. www.shambhala.org

Phyllis Schafer Rodriguez has been involved in community and social justice issues most of her life, with professional experience as a teacher and artist. On September 11, 2001, her thirty-one-year-old son, Greg, died in the attacks on the World Trade Center in New York City where he worked on the 103rd floor. In 2006, her story appeared on The Forgiveness Project website, a London-based organization that promotes non-vengeful responses to violence through a traveling exhibit called The F Word. After meeting Father Michael Lapsley in 2006, and attending a healing of memories workshop, Phyllis began volunteering for the institute to help bring its work to North America. She also works with The Guantanamo/ Rule of Law Committee of Peaceful Tomorrows, which was formed in response to policies and issues in our nation justified by the "war on terror," a direct outcome of the attacks. Phyllis is active in the committee and has been especially outspoken since spending a week at Guantanamo Bay Naval Base observing pretrial hearings in the death penalty case against Khalid Sheik Mohammed, along with members of four other victims' families chosen by lottery in January 2013. Phyllis is a native New Yorker and product of the New York City public schools, including City College of New York where she met her husband, Orlando Rodriguez. Phyllis Rodriguez lives in New York. www. peacefultomorrows.org

Shantum Seth is an ordained teacher (Dharmacharya) in the Zen Buddhist lineage (of the venerable Thich Nhat Hanh) and has been leading pilgrimages "In the Footsteps of the Buddha" and other multifaith and transformative journeys since 1988. Shantum is actively involved in social, environmental, and educational programs, including work on teacher training through Cultivating Mindfulness in Education, being pioneered by the nonprofit trust, Ahimsa. he is a consultant to the World Bank and the International Finance Corporation to help promote Buddhist circuit tourism in India and is on the advisory board to the Minister of Culture, Government of India. He worked in the corporate sector and later in social advocacy and development, fifteen years of which were with the United Nations Development Programme, managing programs on volunteer promotion and artisan support across sixteen countries, and also initiating the Endogenous Tourism program in India. He has contributed to a number of books including, *Walking with the Buddha, Planting Seeds... Sharing Mindfulness with Children*, and VOLUNTEERS AGAINST CONFLICT. He has also been a consultant on films including "Life of the Buddha" made by the BBC and Discovery and "The Story of India" made by BBC and PBS. Shantum Seth studied at The Doon School and St. Stephen's College in India and then graduated in Development Studies with his thesis in Gandhian Economics from the University of East Anglia in England. His commitment to a cross-cultural and global understanding has led him to travel to more than fifty countries and nearly every state of India. Shantum Seth lives in India. www.buddhapath.com

Cathrine Sneed began the horticulture program for prisoners in the San Francisco County Jail in 1982. Early in the jail's history, which was built in 1934, the facility grew its own food. Cathrine and the prisoners worked to transform the abandoned buildings and fields into a farm that would grow organic vegetables for homeless shelters and soup kitchens—a job training program that used horticulture as a metaphor for personal growth while benefiting poor communities. Prisoners responded favorably to the program; however, upon release, they faced many challenges. Many of the participants in the horticulture program continued to return to jail. Taking the lessons from that program, Cathrine and San Francisco Sheriff Michael Hennessey worked to create a program that would affect the high rates of recidivism and continue the work of the horticulture program in communities in San Francisco Cathrine Sneed lives in Northern California.

THE KARUNA CENTER was established as a way of helping individuals, communities, and organizations find ways to live and work in ways that do not harm others or the planet. Our mission is to cultivate our shared humanity and collective responsibility for a more just, kind and compassionate world by supporting social impact groups, building resilient communities, and making conflict generative and transformative.

Learn more: www.thekarunacenter.org

CPSIA information can be obtained
at www.ICGtesting.com
Printed in the USA
BVHW071602210521
607866BV00004B/727